THE SECRET POWER OF JURIES

What jurors in Canada aren't told about their rights — and what we can do about it

Gary Bauslaugh

James Lorimer & Company Ltd., Publishers
Toronto

ADVANCE PRAISE FOR *THE SECRET POWER OF JURIES*

"The secret is out. Jurors are now told by Gary Bauslaugh about their rights and perhaps with the publication of this important book, juries will know that they can continue to have the right to do what the law sometimes fails to do — deliver justice."

— from the Foreword by Morris Manning, Q.C., C.S., J.D.

"Gary Bauslaugh brings an important and troubling legal issue to the people of Canada so they can judge how well (or how poorly) the jury system copes with injustice. Written with clarity, and truly engaging the reader."

— Clayton Ruby, C.M., LL.D.

"For those interested in the power of the jury, this book is a thought-provoking analysis of a troubling question."

— Edward L. Greenspan, Q.C.

"This book deserves praise for raising critical questions many seem to want kept permanently secret."

— Justin Trottier, activist and host of *Think Again! TV*

James Lorimer & Company Ltd., Publishers acknowledges the support of the Ontario Arts Council. We acknowledge the financial support of the Government of Canada through the Canada Book Fund for our publishing activities. We acknowledge the support of the Canada Council for the Arts which last year invested $24.3 million in writing and publishing throughout Canada. We acknowledge the Government of Ontario through the Ontario Media Development Corporation's Ontario Book Initiative.

Cover design: Tyler Cleroux
Cover image: shutterstock

Library and Archives Canada Cataloguing in Publication

Bauslaugh, Gary, author
        The secret power of juries : what jurors in Canada aren't told about their rights—and what we can do about it / Gary Bauslaugh.

Includes bibliographical references and index.
Issued in print and electronic formats.
ISBN 978-1-4594-0505-9 (pbk.).--ISBN 978-1-4594-0506-6 (epub)

        1. Jury—Canada. 2. Jurors—Canada. I. Title.

KE8495.B39 2013   347.71'0752   C2013-904164-8
KF8972 B39 2013   C2013-904165-6

James Lorimer & Company Ltd., Publishers
317 Adelaide Street West, Suite 1002
Toronto, Ontario, Canada
M5V 1P9
www.lorimer.ca

Printed and bound in Canada.

CONTENTS

There is a higher court than courts of justice and that is the court of conscience. It supersedes all other courts.

Mohandas Gandhi

I have always found that mercy bears richer fruits than strict justice.

Abraham Lincoln

It is not what a lawyer tells me I may do; but what humanity, reason and justice tell me I ought to do.

Edmund Burke

FOREWORD

The secret is out. Jurors are now told by Gary Bauslaugh about their rights, and perhaps with the publication of this important book, juries will know that they can continue to have the right to do what the law sometimes fails to do — deliver justice.

While the topic is arcane, its importance cannot be overstated. Since the Magna Carta, jurors have had the right to do justice under the law and, equally important, to do justice in accordance with their own conscience. *The Secret Power of Juries* points out a pattern of jury nullification in court cases for over 100 years, and illustrates cases where the pattern of jury nullification yields justice and where the strict application of the law would yield up injustice. Jurors in Canada, as a result of the comments by the Supreme Court of Canada in the *Morgentaler* case, are not allowed to be told that they have this power.

This book is not only a viable contribution to the literature dealing with juries and the judicial system but it is also very readable and interesting. The wealth of information gained from previous cases is informative. The analysis of jury nullification and the cases of *Latimer* and *Morgentaler* are proper illustrations of the point that the author makes — jury nullification should not be kept secret. The analysis of Chief Justice Dickson's reasons for denying juries the right to know the law, and the resulting impact on cases such as *Latimer,* demonstrate the reach and hardship caused by the ruling.

The entirety of the book lays out the pros and cons of jury nullification and readers should come to the conclusion, for the reasons set out in the rebuttal of Chief Justice Dickson's analysis of jury nullification, that their power should no longer be kept secret.

No rights or powers given to public figures in the justice system — be they legislators, lawyers or appointed judges — should be kept secret, particularly from those lay judges: the jury. It should not be an offence for a lawyer to tell the jury they have the power to find a verdict against the law and the power to find a verdict against the evidence. The legislators know the law because they make the law. The lawyers know the law because they interpret the law. The judges know the law because they are applying the law. Therefore, there is no reason why jurors, who are told to apply the law and to judge a person in accordance with their conscience, should not also know the law, which includes their right to know their powers.

It is ironic that notwithstanding the fact that we are the only major democratic country to allow an appeal by the prosecutor against a jury acquittal, we have also sought to foreclose lawyers being able to tell jurors what their powers are. The secret does not need to be kept secret where appellate courts can and do intervene, as seen by the *Morgentaler* case itself. A copy of this book should be in every room where prospective jurors are called for jury duty.

— Morris Manning, Q.C., C.S., J.D.

Manning is certified as a specialist in criminal litigation by the Law Society of Upper Canada. As a criminal lawyer, he has prosecuted cases at trial level courts and argued appeals before all levels of court. Manning was counsel for Henry Morgentaler during his 1983 trial.

PREFACE

Why should we care about the law? Much of the time it seems irrelevant to our lives, at best, and a serious nuisance or impediment to our lives at worst. Most of us do not often reflect on how central it is to our well-being. Civilized life as we know it would not be possible without an effective system of rule by law.

In his recent book, *The Rule of Law,* British lawyer Tom Bingham defines the core principle of law as follows:

> *That all persons and authorities within the state, whether public or private, should be bound by and entitled to the benefit of laws publicly made . . . and publicly administered in the courts.*

This dry and seemingly simple statement leads to a vast array of complex, complementary legal principles that form the basis of what we call our justice system. Does this justice system always lead to justice? Sadly no, but it is not for want of trying. The principles that have emerged are for the most part meant to build a justice system that is truly just, but humans are so diverse, and human interactions so complex, that laws cannot capture the myriad of possibilities that inevitably arise in any legal jurisdiction.

So, at times, the justice system leads to what most would call injustice.

What remedies do we have? We can go back to some of the core principles of law that Bingham discusses — principles seeking fairness and justice — and examine when and how these sometimes go wrong:

1) THE LAW MUST BE THE SAME FOR EVERYONE

This basic principle has been part of English law and subsequently legal systems based on English law (such as ours) since 1215, when the Magna Carta proclaimed that kings and noblemen should be subject to the same laws as everyone else. This idea — that state officials are not above the law — is one that we accept without question today, but it was a radical concept in 1215.

This is not to say that, in reality, the law is equally applied to all. If one is charged with a criminal offence, or, for that matter, a civil offence, it is very helpful indeed to be rich. And it is very risky to be poor and, worse, to be a member of an identifiable minority. This shameful aspect of our legal system is not, however, by design but arises as an unfortunate by-product of an economic system in which money talks and poverty is (for the most part) silent.

A stark example of this, in the United States, occurred in the infamous prosecution of the West Memphis Three (see Chapter Notes). As the mother of one of the wrongly convicted boys said:

The damn system stinks . . . If we had money, you think these three boys would've been picked up? They found people they knew didn't have money . . . But they're wrong. They're bad wrong.

This sort of injustice, sadly, is not unknown in most legal jurisdictions. In Canada, our legal system has good intentions in regard to equality. Our *Charter of Rights and Freedoms* asserts "fundamental freedoms" guaranteed for all and that "every individual is equal before the law," and most Canadians strongly support these principles. But in practice, in the sort of society in which we live, inequalities in application of the law are commonplace.

That is not to suggest we should passively accept inequalities in the application of law. These inequalities are contrary to the principles of law we value. We are, therefore, morally obliged to seek equality in application of the law wherever and whenever we can.

At the same time we know that judges and juries will not always be perfectly consistent: they will not always return the same verdicts in the same circumstances. Different people, in good faith, will sometimes come to different conclusions; that is something we cannot and should not try to regulate. Human judgment will always entail some degree of variability. What we can do, though, insofar as it is possible, is ensure that all those entrusted with coming to a verdict have the same basic information.

In the interests of seeking equal treatment under the law, it would seem reasonable that, at the minimum, all juries should be provided with the same information — that all should be equally aware of their powers. This seemingly innocuous position is, as you will see in this book, a matter of serious contention.

2) THE LAW MUST BE ACCESSIBLE

In regard to laws publicly made and publicly administered, Bingham writes, "if you and I are liable to be prosecuted, fined and perhaps imprisoned for doing or failing to do something, we ought to be able, without undo difficulty, to find out what it is we must or must not do . . ."

The *Criminal Code of Canada* and the *Charter of Rights and Freedoms* do make most aspects of the law quite clear; they (especially the *Charter*) do not get too bogged down in incomprehensible legal language. Those who drafted these documents deserve credit for that.

There are some aspects of law, however, that are less clear and less accessible. Sometimes a law is not clearly enunciated but is based on decisions of previous courts; this is called case law or common law. Such law is less accessible and often requires legal searches and legal analysis.

The prevailing principle, however, as Bingham argues, ought to be accessibility of law, wherever and whenever it is relevant and possible. It would seem indefensible to keep relevant legal facts away from any participant in legal proceedings.

As you will also see in this book, however, this too is a matter of some contention.

3) THE LAW MUST BE FAIR AND EXERCISED IN A FAIR MANNER

Any law can be abused by improper execution. As Bingham puts it:

> *Ministers and public officers at all levels must exercise the powers conferred upon them in good faith, fairly, for the purpose for which the powers were conferred . . .*

This would not seem to be a contentious position, except that a problem arises in the interpretation of the ideas of fairness. For some, fairness — justice — is simply rigid application of the law.

An extreme example of this is aptly found in a quote attributed to American Supreme Court Justice Antonin Scalia:

Mere factual innocence is no reason not to carry out a death sentence properly reached.

"Factual innocence" here means actual innocence. This quote may not be fully accurate (see Chapter Notes), but if he did not use those exact words Scalia has at other times showed an undue reverence for legal procedures. For some, the adherence to proper procedures is the essence of fairness.

An American black man, Benjamin Spencer, has been in prison since 1987 for the murder of a white businessman, even though in 2008 he was declared "factually innocent" by a Dallas judge. It is as though factual innocence is somehow not real innocence, when stacked up against the outcome of proper courtroom procedures.

Such casual dismissals of the relevance of the truth in seeking fairness in the administration of justice are, admittedly, extreme examples. But they highlight a discord in the understanding of the word "fair." Rigorously sticking to proper legal procedures is one idea of fairness. In the first chapter of this book I shall discuss another.

4) EVERY PERSON HAS THE RIGHT TO A FAIR TRIAL

Bingham calls this "a cardinal requirement of rule by law." He describes various requirements of such fairness, such as the presumption of innocence and the rules for presenting evidence. He describes the absolute necessity of "the independence of judicial decision-makers" by which he means "all those making decisions of a judicial character" including judges and jurors.

Bingham writes about the need for judicial decision-makers to be independent of all external influences: politicians, the media, and pressure groups of any kind. He does not, however, address another kind of independence: independence from the law in the interests of a fair outcome.

Judges do not often stray far from the law; they are generally not inclined to do so, and if they inadvertently happen to do so they are likely to have their actions successfully appealed. They have some latitude in selecting and interpreting case law, but they will not and cannot disregard the law altogether (unless the law itself is found to be in violation of the *Charter of Rights and Freedoms*).

But what of juries? Do they, in rendering their verdicts, need to follow the law? Can they find a clearly, even admittedly, guilty defendant, not guilty? Or a proven innocent one guilty?

It is mostly kept secret, but juries can indeed do these things. The practice is called jury nullification. Is this a good thing? Does this serve the cause of fairness in trials? Should it be abolished? If not, should it be kept secret?

This matter concerning the powers and independence of juries is, as you will see, a contentious issue indeed.

* * *

The first chapter of this book explains how I became interested in the matter of jury independence as it relates to justice, and clarifies some of the terms used. The second chapter shows how the practice of jury nullification has been a factor in some well-known trials in Canada and in several other countries. Chapter 3 looks at the origins of jury independence.

Chapters 4 to 6 look at a particular sequence of events involving the trials of Henry Morgentaler and Robert Latimer that have led to a serious legal problem with suppression of jury independence in Canada.

The final chapters examine the arguments for and against jury independence and offer suggestions for what we should do about this odd, unresolved, and important social and legal matter.

CHAPTER 1

A BOOK ON . . . JURY NULLIFICATION?

Jury nullification just sounds like something bad. When I mentioned it to a group of friends, a rather well turned-out woman thought I said "jewelry nullification." "No one is taking away my jewels," she said. A gentleman in the group, a rather serious and socially concerned one, thought I had said "Jewry nullification." He made some dark comment about anti-Semitism.

At that point I began to realize what a task I had ahead of me. Writing and selling a book on a topic no one knows anything about was not going to be easy. I hadn't known anything much about it myself before writing a book in 2010 about the famous Canadian mercy killing case of Robert Latimer. I had heard of jury nullification but really did not know what it meant. But it turned out to be a matter central to the Latimer case: he went to prison largely because his jury did not know much about it either.

I discovered that not only was Latimer's fate probably a consequence of his jury's being unaware of jury nullification, but there were also important, larger, long-standing and unresolved legal and philosophical issues surrounding the idea. There was something worth exploring here, if only I could find a way past the reader's inclination to skip over what sounds unpleasant and boring. Jury nullification is actually neither unpleasant nor boring (it just sounds like that). In fact it is a fascinating and important aspect of our justice system that ought to be much more widely understood.

Jury nullification refers to the power of juries to act independently of the law: to come to any verdict they wish, whatever the evidence, whatever the law. Juries can nullify the law. It should be noted that nullification is the deliberate contravening of the law by the jury: knowingly coming to a verdict that is contrary to the verdict prescribed by law.

It is not nullification if a jury simply does not believe the evidence; evaluating the evidence is the jury's traditional role. The jury members might get it right or they might get it wrong, but if they use their evaluation of the evidence to come to a verdict, that is not nullification. It is nullification only when, despite the jury's belief that the evidence points to guilt or innocence, it renders the opposite verdict.

Latimer's jury was a sympathetic one: his jury members clearly thought that anything more than a token penalty would not be appropriate in his case. But instead they came to the verdict they thought they were obliged to come to, a verdict of guilty that inexorably led to a lifetime sentence for Latimer, with a minimum of ten years in prison. Had even one of those jurors happened to understand the power of jury nullification and told the other members about it, there is a good chance Latimer would have been freed and his already long legal ordeal would have ended right then.

The legal system should not, of course be so capricious, with a crucial verdict depending on whether or not jurors happen to know this relatively obscure bit of legal information about their power to nullify. I began to wonder where the idea came from, why more people did not know about it, and why juries were not told about it. There is something worth looking at here, I thought, but where to start?

In the spring of 2012 my wife, Gwyneth, and I were visiting Britain while conducting research on an entirely different writing project. I still had the Latimer case on my mind and continued to be troubled by his jury's lack of information about jury independence. How is this equal treatment under the law, I thought, when some juries will know their powers in regard to making an independent decision, and others will not? How can a man's freedom depend upon such luck-of-the-draw? All that had to happen was for someone — the judge, the defence lawyer — to tell the jury. But for some reason they could not, or would not.

I had mentioned jury nullification in my book on Latimer, but controversies about the right to live and the right to die overshadowed the issue. Maybe a book devoted to the topic would be more effective and bring more attention to the matter. Maybe that, I thought, would be the right thing to do; maybe that would be one small way I could help fight against unequal protection under the law. But, still, how to get anyone interested and where to start?

Gwyneth and I happened to go on a guided tour of the Old City of London. Among the many points of interest on the tour was the Old Bailey courthouse, where the famous 1670 trial of William Penn had taken place and his jury had refused to find him guilty for his defiance of an unjust law. I realized that the story had direct bearing on the matter of jury nullification. I must find out more about the Penn trial, I thought.

A few nights later, by chance, we stayed for a night at the Penn Club, a hotel run by Quakers in the Bloomsbury district of London. Penn was a Quaker and is a hero of that movement. We had been staying at another hotel in the same area, but due to a scheduling error we had to move out for one night, and found a vacancy at the Penn Club. We had actually stayed there once or twice in the past and had found it pleasant and well run and were amused by the quaint rule asking guests not to consume alcohol in their rooms. We always acceded to the hotel's wishes.

This time, as we checked in, an antique embroidery sampler hanging on the lobby wall caught Gwyneth's eye. It was a celebration of William

Penn's stand against the repressive laws against religious freedom during the reign of King Charles II. It told of how Penn's jury members refused to convict him, even though they were fined and imprisoned themselves for not coming up with a verdict of guilty.

This second chance encounter with the story of Penn and his jury members inspired me to think that I had to move ahead with this project. Jury nullification was alive and well in 1670, but now, at least in the case of the Latimer trial over 340 years later, it seemed almost like some sort of wicked secret, not to be mentioned in court or anywhere else. Why was that?

A DANGEROUS IDEA?

I had noticed a distinct lack of interest in jury nullification when I wrote my book about Latimer, even though it seemed to be a key point in the Latimer trials. Alan Borovoy, the eminent Canadian civil libertarian, in an otherwise complimentary review, wrote that he recommended the book "despite some differences over the points Gary Bauslaugh has chosen to emphasize." He was referring to my comments about nullification and the central role it played, or could have played, in the Latimer trials. John Dixon, philosopher and prominent member of the BC Civil Liberties Association, also wrote some very positive comments about the book but told me he disagreed with the emphasis on nullification.

These are very smart people for whom I have much respect. Could they have a point? Was there good reason for antipathy toward jury nullification?

Feelings about open discussion of nullification can get very strong. In December 2011, Julian Heicklen, an 80-year-old political activist, was arrested on the plaza outside the federal courthouse in Manhattan for distributing certain pamphlets to those passing by. Were the pamphlets seditious — that is, were they counselling some sort of illegal action against the state? It hardly seemed so. Was Heicklen advocating hatred? No, not that either. Were the pamphlets at least untrue? Again, no. He was just distributing truthful information available to anyone on the Internet.

Julian Heicklen was distributing pamphlets that provided information about a jury's power to nullify the law. The New York City police viewed this as an action so dangerous, they arrested Heicklen. Heicklen was informing people that, whatever the law says about a particular case, whatever a judge or defence lawyers or prosecutors happen to say, juries are fully independent when it comes to rendering a verdict.

This was accurate information; Heicklen was right. But the authorities did not want him telling anyone about it. Is jury nullification such a dangerous idea that people have to be arrested for giving out information about it?

There have been many times in history when particular bits of knowledge have been deemed too dangerous or unseemly for human consumption. Knowledge about making nuclear weapons, for example, has been and would still be considered something that ought not to be made available to everyone. But opposition to most other kinds of knowledge seems questionable. Certain sexual practices such as homosexuality were once considered so heinous that there was little mention of them in polite circles; it was considered preferable to pretend they did not exist, I suppose in part because of hopes that the ideas would not spread. This was once forbidden knowledge, although now for most of the Western world it is not.

Today it seems that information about jury nullification is forbidden knowledge. Maybe, then, there is something dangerous about the idea. Maybe the critics of jury nullification are right, and promoting information about this power of juries, accurate though it may be, can be legitimately construed as harmful to society and to the state. Maybe, if they are right, Julian Heicklen's act was an act of sedition. Maybe writing this book is, too. Reading it might be risky as well — fair warning!

I do not, however, mean to make light of a complex issue. There are real risks with jury independence, as you will see in some of the cases in

Chapter 2. Jury independence, leading to jury nullification, has allowed murderers to go free, even vicious, racist ones. Should jurors have this power and be allowed to decide if a law, in a particular case, ought to be followed? We know that conscience is flawed. We know jurors can be wrong. We know jurors might not appreciate the intricacies of the law they are dealing with. So maybe it is best to encourage them to just go along with the verdict that is directed by law.

Many people in the legal community, especially judges and prosecutors, question the practice of jury independence and nullification. They recognize the obvious injustice of applying the law in certain cases, but they argue this is the price we pay for a system of rule by law. We must be ruled by laws, they say, not by the fickle and inexpert opinions of lay people.

Nullification itself, mind you, is within the law; it is not illegal to come to a verdict that is contrary to law. But practicing nullification means that a jury is denying the application of some other particular law, a denial made by lay people in the face of either legislated laws or laws derived from previous legal decisions (common law). In either case substantial and considered legal thinking has gone into the making of a law. Is it right that lay people trifle with this? It is legal for them to do so, but is it right?

Most judges in most trials think not. Thus we see them lecturing juries on the need to find a verdict that is in accord with the law and refusing to allow them to be informed (and in some cases even deceiving them) about their power to nullify. We see prosecutors excluding jurors they suspect might know about nullification. We see events like the arrest of Julian Heicklen for publicly distributing information about the power to nullify.

So should jury independence be openly encouraged, or is the majority of the legal community right in wanting to suppress it? Where do you stand? At this point I suggest only that you read through the rest of this book before deciding.

JUSTICE AND THE LAW

Frequently in this book I use the words "justice" and "law." These are words that are sometimes conflated: "bringing a person to justice" is an expression often used to say that the law is being applied to that person. This overlap in meaning is reinforced by some dictionary definitions of justice such as "the exercise of authority in maintenance of right." The justice system is what we call our laws and our means for enforcing those laws.

But there is a broader meaning to the word "justice": that which is right rather than that which the law dictates. If the law says it is all right to waterboard prisoners to extract information from them, is such a position in fact right? Does that represent any sort of justice, in the broader sense of the term? When the Nazis legally persecuted the Jews, is there any way we can sensibly call the system that allowed such atrocities a "justice system," except in the most technical sense?

So for purposes of the discussion in this book we will separate the meanings of these words: the law is that which is set down in statutes and regulations or which arises from earlier precedents (common law); justice refers to that which we understand to be right.

The *Canadian Charter of Rights and Freedoms* alludes to this separation of the meanings of justice:

> **Section 7.** *Everyone has the right to life, liberty and security of the person and the right not to be deprived thereof except in accordance with the principles of fundamental justice.*

The phrase "the administration of justice" is used in Section 24, referring to the official actions of the representatives of the justice system. Section 7 clearly refers to a different sort of justice, a "fundamental justice" that suggests an overriding importance to doing what is right.

But how do we determine what is right? We can easily read the *Criminal Code* and determine what our criminal law says, but if we want to see justice in some larger sense, in the sense of what is right, how can we determine that?

It seems that most people have an innate moral sense that we call conscience (or, as philosophers like to say, moral intuition). There is, as Gandhi said, a "court of conscience" that "supersedes all other courts." Many of us would oppose torture and racial persecution regardless of what the laws might say. Our consciences would demand that we do so.

Gandhi's "court of conscience" is our internal mechanism for assessing what is right. It is imperfect, to be sure, but it is the one guide we have, other than the law (or other rules of conduct, for example, religious ones) for determining what we ought to do. When conscience — our personal view of right — is in accord with the law, we say that justice has prevailed. And when the two are not in accord, we say that an injustice has occurred.

But conscience is not always a reliable guide to what is right. Conscience is influenced by many different factors, not only positive moral learning that might come from families, schools, and religious teachings, and today by the media, but also from prejudices and facile and ignorant ideas that may be passed on by these same sources and which may be harmful to society. What seems like conscience may have nothing to do with justice.

At the same time, conscience is not to be lightly dismissed. There seems to be a basic aspect of the human conscience that overrides teachings. Humans have an innate and fundamental concern for fairness — for justice — that can prevail over the various and frequently dubious moral claims to which we are constantly subjected. There is a natural empathy in humans: we care about one another; we feel each other's pain and suffering. We react against unfairness not only when it is inflicted upon us but also when it happens to other people. This is not universal: psychopaths seem not to care at all about others, and demagogic leaders can sometimes lead otherwise decent people to do terrible things. But for most people in most circumstances, conscience remains a powerful force. (Refer to Chapter Notes for a more detailed observation on this.)

Mark Twain dramatizes these different aspects of conscience in one of the most memorable episodes of *Huckleberry Finn*. Huck helps his friend Jim, a runaway slave, evade capture. Huck is then wracked by guilt, feeling he will go to Hell for having broken the law and the codes of his slave-owning Southern society. Twain elsewhere refers to this as a circumstance where "a sound heart and a deformed conscience came into collision and conscience suffers defeat." Huck's sound heart is the natural, empathetic sort of conscience; his deformed conscience is one learned in a bigoted society.

Officials of the state — police, prosecutors, politicians, judges — are somewhat insulated from the effects of empathetic conscience, because they are engaged in formulating and enforcing laws that will govern all of society. They are focused on rules and on building an orderly and controlled society, and it is generally a good thing that they are. But most of them would have turned Jim in with hardly a second thought. They would have been convinced by what they had been taught: that it was right to do so, right always to follow society's rules. Huck, though, while still indoctrinated by societal biases, had enough humanity to let the empathetic side of him triumph.

Those responsible for enforcing the law are conditioned and more-or-less obligated to serve the law at all costs. This is normally what their consciences tell them is right. If Robert Latimer took the life of his daughter, they say, then he is a murderer and should be treated as such. We expect this from officials; that is what they have been trained to think is right. To them, justice is essentially the same thing as the application of law. Conscience drives such people not toward a broader conception of justice but to enforce laws. Their consciences are not "deformed" but focused on society and its needs, not on individual circumstances. Their justice, official justice, is one that preserves and protects society's rules.

The Latimer case, however, brought out the Huck Finn in millions of ordinary people. It brought out the empathetic conscience, not the deformed one and not the official one. Millions of us, including those sitting on his jury, felt that murder was too harsh a charge for what was intended as an act of human kindness and mercy. This application of the "justice system" — the law — was, to us, an injustice.

Officials will see justice in the orderly application of rules: official justice. Bigots will see it in some sort of deformed way. But others will see it according to the dictates of empathetic conscience. This conscience will allow us to feel — no, it will insist that we feel — what it is like to be in another person's shoes. It will lead to the demand for fairness and humane justice.

One generally acknowledged value of an independent jury of peers — the subject of this book — is that it takes judgment away from lawmakers and puts it into the hands of ordinary people, people who are not wedded to the sanctity of process and the law. Such jurors can view the circumstances of a trial not from the conditioned perspective of a law-enforcer but from the point of view of empathetic fellow humans. They provide a chance for conscience — the good kind — to prevail.

TO NULLIFY OR NOT TO NULLIFY?

So which view of juries should prevail: that they consist of ordinary people with consciences who can and should take an independent, empathetic view of a case, or, as suggested earlier, that they are inexpert lay people who should not presume to challenge laws they may not even understand? Is the secret power of juries — the power to nullify the law — better suppressed, or should it be out in open view? Is it proper or even safe (remember Julian Heicklen) to talk about it?

I invite you to take a chance and explore these questions with me. Four months after his arrest, the charges against Heicklen were dismissed. So maybe it is quite safe to read on.

CHAPTER 2

A MIXED HISTORY OF JURY NULLIFICATION

In most countries with legal systems based on English law, juries have the power to act independently in the sense that they are fully entitled to come to any verdict they wish, regardless of what the law says. When they knowingly come to a verdict contrary to the law, such action is called jury nullification.

Historically, this power of juries has led to both desirable and undesirable outcomes. Does the bad outweigh the good, as many believe? Should the power to nullify be suppressed because of the bad? In seeking to answer this question let us first examine a number of famous cases involving nullification.

Note: some readers may question the absence of arguably the most famous case of all, that of O.J. Simpson. This reason it is left out is that it is not a clear case of jury nullification. Nullification is when the jury agrees with one fiew of the evidence but chooses not to abide by what the law says should come of it. It is not clear that Simpson's jury thought he was guilty; as odd as it might seem, they may have thought him to be not guilty. In that case they would not be nullifying the law but going with the law: innocent unless proven guilty. This jury, because of inept prosecutors and very skilled defence lawyers, may well have been persuaded that Simpson was innocent. More details about this strange case are given in the Chapter Notes.

JOHN PETER ZENGER – COLONIAL NEW YORK, 1734

Zenger arrived in New York, from Germany, in his early teens. He worked in a print shop for several years before opening his own shop in 1726. In 1733 he started the *New York Weekly Journal*, the second newspaper in the area, the other being the *Gazette*, published by Zenger's former employer.

While the *Gazette* was effectively under the control of the royal governor, William Cosby, who was appointed by the king, the *Weekly Journal* was independent and fiercely critical. It relentlessly attacked Cosby and the Cosby administration. Zenger did not write or edit the offending articles, but as publisher he was legally responsible for them.

Cosby, who had arrived from Britain in 1731, was a very unpopular governor. Historians have not been flattering in their descriptions of him, using such adjectives as haughty, spiteful, and quick-tempered. He ruled the colony with a firm hand and was not about to brook public criticism. On November 17, 1734, Cosby had Zenger arrested for seditious libel and held in prison for eight months before the trial started. The paper missed publication for only one day, however, as Zenger's wife, Anna, took over the operation. Bail for Zenger was set at an impossible 800 pounds; however, this and other punitive actions by the governor served to further inflame public opinion against him.

Zenger had two friendly lawyers working on his behalf, lawyers who had helped defend the newspaper during earlier skirmishes, but they were debarred by the Cosby administration. A pro-Cosby lawyer was initially appointed to defend Zenger, but soon the famous trial lawyer Andrew Hamilton from Philadelphia took over.

Jury selection started on July 29, 1735. Cosby tried to stack the jury with his supporters, but even the two judges in the case, handpicked by Cosby, objected to this irregularity. The judges then ensured that twelve untainted jurors were selected. The trial itself began on August 4. The prosecutor argued that Zenger was a "seditious person" who had wickedly and maliciously tried to "traduce, scandalize and vilify" Governor Cosby and his administration.

Hamilton rose to speak. He astonished the court by announcing that his client would not deny having printed the allegedly libellous materials and that in doing so he would save the prosecution the trouble of trying to establish this point. This was contrary to the defence in previous libel trials, which would involve somehow denying that the libel had happened as described or claiming that the defendant was in some way not responsible for it. But Hamilton had another plan. He was going to appeal directly to the jury on the grounds that the law was wrong to count as libel anything negative said about someone. Hamilton would argue that it is not libel if what is written is true. This had not been argued before.

The prosecutor then argued that since there had now been a confession, all that was left was for the jury to find Zenger guilty. Hamilton was undeterred and continued his argument by stating that the libel law of England ought not to be the libel law of New York. Knowing this argument would immediately appeal to those becoming dissatisfied with English rule, he said:

> I hope Mr. Attorney will not think it proper to apply his law cases, to support the cause of his governor, which have only been judged where the king's safety and honor was concerned . . .

In other words, English libel law was made to protect the honour of the king, and the governor is no king. All of this would be immensely appealing to citizens of the colonies. This was not England. Why should the governor have the protection meant for a king?

This was an appealing argument but there was no obvious legal justification for it — not for having different libel laws in New York and not for truth as a defence. The law as it stood was on the prosecutor's side. But Hamilton's strategy was to convince the jurors that the law was wrong and therefore should not be followed. He was asking the jury to exercise its power to nullify a bad law.

The prosecutor argued that the only role for the jury was to determine if Zenger had printed and published the offending documents, something Zenger had already admitted. The determination of what was libellous, the prosecutor argued, was up to the judge.

Hamilton said the jury certainly *could* do what the prosecutor said they must do, but they could also do otherwise. They could determine the facts in a case and take the law from the judge, as is customary and as the prosecutor was arguing, or they themselves could decide what the law should be:

> I know that they [the jury members] have the right beyond all dispute to determine both the law and the fact . . .

To limit juries in the way the prosecutor wanted to limit them, according to Hamilton, "renders juries useless."

Hamilton then presented an eloquent and compelling argument for a free press, as justification for why the jury should not follow the existing law. I will include one excerpt here:

> Power may justly be compared to a great river. While kept within its due bounds it is both beautiful and useful. But when it overflows its banks, it is then too impetuous to be stemmed; it bears down all before it, and brings destruction and desolation wherever it comes. If, then, this is the nature of power, let us at least do our duty, and like wise men who value freedom use our utmost care to support liberty, the only bulwark against lawless power, which in all ages

has sacrificed to its wild lust and boundless ambition the blood of the best men that ever lived . . .

The two judges did not know what to do except to reiterate that the jury's obligation was to follow the law. But after a short deliberation the jury came back with a verdict of "not guilty."

* * *

The trial is best known for being a landmark event in establishing freedom of speech. The law was not immediately rewritten, but libel prosecutions in the colonies, like the prosecution of Zenger, ceased because they would likely meet this newly discovered instrument of social change: jury nullification. Freedom of the press blossomed because of it. That freedom is widely celebrated today. The freedom of juries that led to this great legal victory, however, remains in relative obscurity, suppressed by the legal establishment.

FREDERICK JENKINS, A.K.A. SHADRACH — BOSTON, 1851

One of the ugliest laws ever passed in the United States — maybe the ugliest — was the *Fugitive Slave Act* of 1850. It was signed into law by President Millard Fillmore, one of the least distinguished of American presidents. The *Act*, replacing an earlier, weaker one, allowed slave hunters almost complete freedom to hunt down and apprehend runaway slaves, even in free states. Any United States marshal who did not fully assist was subject to a hefty fine. Suspected escaped slaves were summarily captured and returned, with little recourse to any legal assistance.

Anyone assisting a runaway, including those runaways who made it to free states, was also subject to heavy fines and imprisonment. Sometimes marshals would capture free blacks in the North, claiming they were runaways, and then sell them to slave owners in the South.

On February 14, 1851, Frederick Jenkins, a black man working as a hotel waiter in Boston, was arrested under the *Fugitive Slave Act*. He had escaped from a slave-owner in Virginia about nine months earlier. While the case was being heard in a Boston courtroom, with Jenkins facing the prospect of being sent to the slave owner, a large number of sympathizers, black and white, rushed the courtroom and swept the defendant away and out of the city and the state and eventually into Canada. He settled in Montreal, married an Irish woman, and found work operating a restaurant.

Eight of the rescuers, four black and four white, were arrested, and three went to trial on May 27, 1851. The trial would go on for three weeks but was then suspended because of disagreements amongst the jurors, and then all charges were dropped. No convictions were ever made in this case, despite the fact that prosecutors, judges, and even President Fillmore pushed for convictions. The president and the federal government were anxious to reassure Southerners that they were serious about enforcing the *Fugitive Slave Act*. The jury, though, refused to co-operate despite the obvious lawlessness of the action the defendants had taken.

One of the black defendants was Robert Morris, a lawyer himself. His lawyer argued that the jury should not judge him personally for what he did, but instead blame the law that caused people to commit such acts. He said that if any of the jurors believed that the *Fugitive Slave Act* was unconstitutional they should disregard any instructions by the judge to the contrary. The judge, the eminent Supreme Court Justice Benjamin Curtis, made a strong argument against this advice to jurors, saying:

> *To enforce popular laws is easy. But when an unpopular cause is a just cause, when a law unpopular in some locality, is to be enforced there, then comes the strain upon the administration of justice . . .*

Curtis's position was that, though it could be difficult to enforce at times, the law is the law and cannot be different in different places. But

Massachusetts was not Mississippi. It still is not. White citizens of Massachusetts, sitting on the jury, refused to support a racist law and convict the men, white and black, who were in violation of that law.

* * *

There were other acts of defiance against the *Fugitive Slave Act*, including a number of successful and unsuccessful attempts to forcibly remove runaway slaves from custody. While the federal government and the president were engaged in placating a rebellious South, the Northern free states were not so encumbered. Individuals and even some law enforcement authorities showed great bravery in refusing to co-operate with a politically expedient but fundamentally immoral law.

The bold rescue of Jenkins and the subsequent refusal of the jury to convict the rescuers was an example of how the power of jury nullification can be used against laws that violate community standards of justice.

THE DONNELLYS – ONTARIO, 1880

Sometime in the 1930s — no one can remember exactly when — an old woman entered the police station on Carling Street in London, Ontario. In a quavering but determined voice she demanded that the police do something about the murders of the Donnelly family. This was the first of several visits she made to that station, always around February 4, always with the same demand: to bring the murderers to justice.

The Donnelly family had indeed been massacred — five of them in one evening — in the nearby Biddulph Township. But the graves had long grown cold by the time the old woman came in to the station demanding justice. The Donnellys had been slaughtered about fifty years earlier, on February 4, 1880! There had been two trials at the time but, in spite of considerable evidence and a detailed eyewitness account of what happened, none of those involved were ever found guilty.

Who was the old woman? Was she a surviving relative or a long-time friend of the Donnellys? She was neither of those. In fact she had probably not seen any Donnelly in something like sixty years. Her name was Maggie Thompson, and she once had been in love with Will Donnelly, second of eight children born to James and Johannah Donnelly. Will (b. 1845) and his older brother James (b. 1842) were born while the Donnellys still lived in Tipperary in Ireland. Famine in Ireland prompted the Donnellys to make the hard emigration to Canada, where they ended up alongside many other Irish immigrants in Biddulph Township in the early 1850s. In Canada the Donnellys had five more sons and then a daughter, Jenny, born in 1858.

Many of the people in the township came from the fractious Tipperary area of Ireland, and they brought with them their habits of religious intolerance and hatred and the practice of forming terrorist cults with sworn oaths of secrecy. There were Protestants, fervently anti-Protestant Catholics, and other Catholics who had the effrontery to consort with Protestants. These two brands of Catholics were the bitterest of enemies, with stronger hatred between them than existed between Catholics and Protestants. The Donnellys were the milder sort of Catholics, so were particularly hated by the more extreme ones.

Sadly, for Will Donnelly and Maggie Thompson, Maggie's father was one of the Donnelly-haters. He said he would rather see his daughter be burned at the stake than marry a Donnelly. Eventually Thompson forced his daughter to marry a young farmer of his choice. Townspeople long remembered Maggie's hysterical weeping as she was swept away from the wedding ceremony by her new husband.

In the many pages written about the Donnellys, Maggie Thompson does not surface again until her appearances at the London police station, long after both her husband and Will Donnelly had died — an old woman with diminished mental capacities, living out a life of unhappiness, still holding onto a thread of a connection with Will and the Donnelly family, urging the police to do something about those unpunished murders.

* * *

The murderers, identified and well-known, escaped punishment because they could not be convicted in that community. Two juries that refused to follow the law let a vicious band of vigilantes go unpunished. This was a gang that had broken into the Donnelly home and brutally slaughtered four family members, later shooting another to death. But the refusal to convict was just one expression of the problems of a dysfunctional community riven with hatred and vendettas imported from Tipperary County.

The details of the actual massacre are fairly well-known because Johnny O'Connor, an eleven-year-old boy who was staying with the Donnellys that night, witnessed the event and somehow lived to tell what happened. A group of about thirty-five vigilantes descended on the Donnelly house just after midnight. According to Johnny O'Connor, Lucan Constable James Carroll entered the unlocked Donnelly house and announced that he had a warrant for their arrest. The rest of the vigilantes waited outside. Carroll somehow got handcuffs on Tom Donnelly, the only son who happened to be at home, and then Carroll roused the rest of the household, which that night were the senior Donnellys, James and Johannah; Johnny O'Connor; and a niece, Bridget, visiting from Ireland. Young Johnny hid under the bed where he and the old man, James, had been sleeping.

At some signal from Carroll the vigilantes swooped in and clubbed the three Donnellys — James, Johannah, and Tom — to death. Then one asked where the girl was. She had run away and hidden upstairs, but was found and killed as well. Johnny thought at one point he had been seen by one of the vigilantes, but if so he may have been forgotten in the bloody melee. The intruders then set fire to the house and left; there was just enough time for Johnny to escape and run to the neighbours.

This was not enough killing for the vigilantes that night. They headed off to the house of Will Donnelly and his wife, Nora, the daughter of another implacable Donnelly-hating family, the Kennedys. Perhaps because Will had wanted to marry a Thompson and then had married a Kennedy, or maybe just because he was the cleverest and most-feared of the Donnellys, Will was a particular target that night. Will and Nora were asleep in their house. They had two houseguests, including one of Will's younger brothers, John Donnelly.

The vigilantes pounded on the door and yelled "fire," a common way to rouse people. As it happened, John was the first to get up and he went to the door. He opened it and was immediately shot down in a volley of bullets. The killers left, thinking they had got Will and probably wanting to spare Nora, whose family members were probably among the vigilantes. John died in a few minutes, but Will survived and lived on until 1897, embittered by the killings and the fact that no one was ever brought to justice.

The Donnellys were undoubtedly a fractious group: the boys were quite wild and two of them, James Jr. and Robert, seem to have been particularly troublesome. But Biddulph Township, with its imported feuds, had many instances of killings, altercations, and burnings that did not involve the Donnellys. They became convenient scapegoats, however, and an unwarranted reputation grew and grew. They had many supporters as well; the lines were drawn in part based on old feuds but also changed as various land disputes and political disagreements occurred.

One can imagine the difficulty of holding an unbiased trial in a community riven by such hatred. Based on inquests in Lucan in Biddulph Township and preliminary hearings in nearby London, six prime suspects, including James Carroll, were held until the trial in the fall of 1880. At the Lucan inquests local townspeople cheered the prisoners when they were brought in. In fact, before the trial a wave of anti-Donnelly sentiment, emanating from its epicenter in London and Lucan, swept through all of Canada. The prevailing feeling was that they deserved what they got. It is hard to understand this today — how the two elderly Donnellys, the young men Tom and John Donnelly, and especially the visiting Irish girl could have deserved what they got — but vigilante justice can have a frightening public appeal. James Carroll was so confident in his release that he had begun planning a lecture tour.

The prosecutors knew it was going to be difficult to get an unbiased local jury in Middlesex County, the area that included London and Biddulph Township. The *London Free Press* had been full of sensational anti-Donnelly stories, many of which were carried in papers across the country. Two affidavits from the prosecutor's office and one from the London Chief of Police asked the presiding judge for a change of venue, but this was countered by petitions from the defence lawyer, the editor of the *London Free Press*, six prominent businessmen, and five of the prisoners! The application for change was turned down.

In October of 1880 James Carroll was the first to be tried. The prosecutor, Aemilius Irving, stood against a team of defence lawyers led by the ruthless and very clever Hugh MacMahon. However, Will Donnelly and Johnny O'Connor proved to be very effective witnesses and Justice Armour's closing remarks to the jury were very supportive of the prosecution. He said that vigilante committees can never be tolerated, and he accepted the evidence of Johnny O'Connor, even though the defence argued that he was too young to be reliable.

It must have been evident to any observer, biased or not, that these men were indeed guilty of this horrible crime, yet only four of the jury members were willing to find them guilty. The others voted for not guilty, except for one who could not make up his mind. It was what is called a hung jury — a jury that cannot come to a unanimous decision.

The second trial started on Monday, January 24, 1881, with Justices Featherston Osler and Matthew Crooks Cameron from Toronto presiding. Again Carroll was the defendant. Unfortunately Cameron, an old Conservative politician, took the lead in making remarks to the jury, and whereas Justice Armour had been helpful to the prosecution, Cameron was not. This bias on the part of the judge was one of a number of things going against the prosecution this time.

The wily MacMahon managed to create some doubt about Johnny O'Connor, partly over some confusion about his age. The boy had apparently been led to believe by his mother that, at the time of the trial, he was twelve, but MacMahon produced evidence showing that he was actually fifteen. This created some doubt about Johnny. Then MacMahon attacked Mrs. O'Connor for going to Toronto to see the Deputy Attorney General to get some money that had been owed the family for living expenses during the trial. MacMahon made it seem like her son's testimony was about money, not the truth. Through all of this the boy himself held up admirably, despite badgering by the defence. He answered questions clearly and quickly and with consistency.

Very damaging, however, was Cameron's agreement with the defence that Johnny O'Connor might have been in such a state of mind during the massacre that his testimony was not to be relied upon. Cameron also continually sustained defence objections and quashed ones from the prosecution.

There could be no reasonable doubt about Johnny's testimony. So great, however, was the prevailing feeling that the Donnellys were wicked and had to be exterminated, a feeling prompted by the press, and so problematic was the sheer number of potential defendants, that the jury found Carroll not guilty. Had he been found guilty and hanged, would the same thing then have happened to all the other potential defendants, maybe another thirty-five? The jury apparently felt that mass hangings would be too great a price for the community to pay for committing an act that was good for the community, even if that act was a massacre!

There were no more trials. The prosecutors felt that if they could not get Carroll, how could they get anyone else? Carroll had been positively identified as the ringleader. But after the verdict was announced he was practically carried out of the courtroom by jubilant supporters. He was wildly cheered by the boisterous crowd, which soon swelled to about a thousand.

Perhaps puffed up by the cheering throng, the jurors, apparently under the illusion that they had done a good thing, went together down to a studio to get a group photograph taken. One juror said that he would not have found Carroll guilty if he had seen him commit the crime. Another is reported to have said that he might have found Carroll guilty if it were not that "such a verdict would have ultimately resulted in the hanging of half a township."

There were great revelries in Lucan, as well, when word reached there. In both London and Lucan, celebrations went far into the night. Local press reports praised the decision, but those further afield were a bit more circumspect. The *Detroit Free Press* wrote:

> *The two ends of Canada differ somewhat. [In British Columbia] four men were hung last week for the murder of one man, while in Ontario one man was acquitted who was shown to have murdered four persons.*

This was a shameful miscarriage of justice, due to community hostility to the victims and also because a clever defence lawyer was able to persuade jurors that it would be all right to find Carroll not guilty, although they all knew he had committed the crime.

* * *

The verdict for James Carroll in his trial of 1881 was a clear case of jury nullification: the jury knew the defendant was guilty of the crime, but it refused to find him so. The law was "nullified." The release of the murderer Carroll, and his henchmen, was a miscarriage of justice. Should juries be allowed such freedom? You must decide, but I suggest you first read about the other cases in the beginning chapters of this book, and then consider the arguments, pro and con, presented in Chapters 7, 8, and 9.

TED, ROSE, AND JACKIE BATES — SASKATCHEWAN, 1933

People died because of the Great Depression of the 1930s. Many committed suicide when they saw they could not afford the basic necessities of life. Some killed themselves out of shame at having to survive on "relief" — government subsistence support for those who had no other means of survival — or charity supplied by friends, family, or some other source. There was much anger about what was taking place: riots broke out, racism flared up, and a few parents, in despair, even killed their children.

Jackie Bates was one of the unfortunate children slain by his parents. In his book on the Depression, Pierre Berton wrote:

> . . . of all the stark tales that illuminate the bitterness of those years, none rends the heart more than the tragedy of Ted Bates, of Glidden, Saskatchewan, and his wife, Rose.

The story is a painful one. After emigrating from England, Ted Bates worked his way across Canada and in the early 1920s became the town butcher in Glidden, Saskatchewan. He had his own shop, which was doing well, and he was affable and well liked. In 1924, Rose Slater, a woman he had met a few years earlier on a trip back to Britain, arrived in Glidden and the two were married immediately.

It sounds like it was never a very happy marriage. Ted was not exactly a sensitive husband: he told Rose that if she had not come over he would have asked his sister to come and do his housework. He drank and gambled. But Rose did get pregnant, and Edward Jack Bates was born in 1925. He was a cheerful and bright boy, and by all accounts his parents doted on him.

Rose, however, became desperately unhappy in the bleak prairie town. She was unhappy with Ted and she felt trapped. Things did not improve as the Depression struck. Now there were severe financial problems as well, and Ted's business was failing. Rose thought Ted was drinking far too much and not tending to work. She wanted to take Jackie and leave Ted and Glidden behind. Ted, however, would not have it.

Feeling that there was no way out, Rose wrote a strange, despairing letter to Ted's sister in England, where she alluded to having been driven to "do what I intend to do . . . the poor kid will be better off and so will I . . . I have just got to end my life and Jacks just because the man I got is an utter bad." She put the letter away and never sent it. It was found later during the investigation of the case.

Rose eventually persuaded Ted to sell the shop, while they could still get something for it, and move to Vancouver. They got some immediate cash from the sale, with more to come when the buyers could afford it (they never could). Ted claimed they had $1,400 when they left Glidden in November of 1932.

But the Depression of course hit Vancouver too, as many people flooded in from the prairies. This placed a great strain on municipal and provincial relief funds. With all these refugees arriving, British Columbia had the highest rate of unemployment in the country at 28 per cent.

Ted tried operating a couple of grocery stores in the southern part of the city, but they both failed. The money was starting to run low by the spring of 1933, but in June, Ted decided to try a third grocery store. By late October he had lost that store as well, and most of his money was gone. Rose was despondent.

Reluctantly, Ted swallowed his pride and went to the Relief office in Vancouver. He was stunned to learn that, because of the influx of poor people, the city had instituted a one-year residency requirement. Ted and Rose would be getting nothing from the city, because they were a few weeks short of the residency requirement. Ted tried the Provincial Relief office but had the same response there. He was told that to get relief he had to go back to Glidden in Saskatchewan.

That was the last thing he wanted to do, and Rose would not hear of it. She would kill herself first, she said, and repeated the threat to friends. She hated the place and could not bear the humiliation of returning penniless.

However, when the Salvation Army offered to purchase train tickets back to Glidden, they reluctantly accepted. They did not know what else to do.

Before they reached Glidden the family got off in Saskatoon, hoping maybe they could stay there. Ted tried the Saskatoon Relief office but again he was turned away. He was again told that he had to go back to Glidden to get any relief money.

It seems to have been then that Ted and Rose, with no options left (except for the unacceptable return to Glidden), came up with the idea of a suicide pact. With a few dollars they scraped up by selling the last of their possessions they rented a car and headed off to the countryside in the general direction of Glidden. But they had no intention of going there. They were on a suicide mission, with the poor, unwitting Jackie included. After some aimless and confused driving, using up a lot of the small amount of gas they had been able to afford, they finally parked by a schoolhouse. They left the motor running and got into the back seat with their son. It was a cold winter night in early December 1933; they probably told Jackie they were going to stay the night there and were leaving the engine on for warmth.

The thing was horribly botched, however. After about an hour the gas ran out. Rose had temporarily fallen unconscious from the fumes but came to and to her horror found that, while she was still alive, Jackie had died. She tried to rouse Ted. He was very weak and groggy, but alive. She pleaded with him to finish her off. He tried but he was too weakened by the fumes. He tried stabbing her with a meat knife but could not pierce her clothes. He clumsily gashed at her neck with a penknife but missed the artery. She put her head down so he could bash her with the car's crank, but he could not hit hard enough to do much damage. They retrieved razor blades from Ted's luggage and each slashed at their own wrists, causing more bleeding but no lethal wounds. Then they just sat there, with their dead son between them, waiting and hoping to die. But before that happened they were discovered.

The authors of the suicide pact lived; the innocent boy died.

Ted and Rose were arrested and charged with first-degree murder. They recovered from their injuries and went to trial on March 20, 1934, in the town of Wilkie, Saskatchewan. The defence lawyer was a wily old Irishman, Harry Ludgate. The lead prosecutor was George Cruise from Saskatoon, assisted by Walter Smyth from Wilkie. The two prosecutors spent a considerable amount of time preparing their case, which looked like a very strong one.

Immediately after being arrested Ted and Rose had both admitted what they had done. Ludgate was able to discredit that evidence by arguing that they were not in a sound frame of mind when they made their confessions. But there was a lot of other evidence that the two had planned and carried out the death of their son. This was clearly first-degree murder.

Ludgate, however, was giving nothing away. There was indisputable evidence that the boy had died from carbon monoxide inhalation. A renowned pathologist, Dr. Frances McGill, had carried out the autopsy and from the telltale pinkness of some of the boy's tissues and a very high level of carbon monoxide in his blood there was no reasonable doubt about this. But Ludgate disputed it.

Ludgate came up with a ludicrous theory that the boy may have undergone sudden death due to an enlarged thymus gland. He got a doctor to claim that, in his opinion, the boy died of "hyperactive thymus poisoning," an ailment that was dubious at the time and has now been entirely discredited. The prosecution was flabbergasted at this audacious defence and brought back an angry Dr. McGill for rebuttal. She pointed out that after ten days, when the boy's blood was tested, there was still 25 to 40 per cent carbon monoxide in his blood. Ten per cent can be fatal.

"Carbon monoxide was the cause of death without any doubt whatsoever," McGill told the courtroom.

Ludgate countered by asking her if she was sure she had not come to this conclusion before leaving Regina, where she was based. He went on to say how "doctors differ and patients lose their lives."

Even though it was pretty clear they had murdered their son, Ted and Rose had two factors in their favour. The first was the jury's knowledge that if found guilty, both would likely hang, and the jury was particularly uncomfortable with sending a woman to hang.

The other factor affecting the trial was the idea that what really killed Jackie Bates was the Great Depression itself. The people of Saskatchewan, and particularly those from Glidden, saw this death as a result of insensitive government policies that had driven Ted and Rose beyond the limit of anyone's tolerance. Any jury was unlikely to let the government hang two people who they believed to be victims of government relief policies.

Not wanting to address the idea of jury nullification directly — the upright citizens on the jury might have rebelled at the suggestion of not following the law — Ludgate instead gave them a pretext for finding Ted and Rose not guilty. Ludgate did this by questioning the cause of death and offering the hyperactive thymus alternative. This was absurd, but it gave the jury something to hang onto to justify its verdict.

In his closing remarks Ludgate made sure the jury understood that a guilty verdict would mean death by hanging for both Ted and Rose. And he raised the issue of conscience, cautioning them that unless they came to the right verdict they might face "sleepless nights when it was too late to correct a mistake."

Ludgate undoubtedly knew his clients were, by law, responsible for the death of their child, but he wanted his jury to believe that the right verdict, in this case, was not guilty.

Cruise knew about the prevailing resentment against government relief policy and that the defendants here would benefit from it. He stressed that this was a painful case and that he too was sympathetic with the defendants, but they all, jury members and prosecutors, had a duty to do. Times were hard, to be sure, but that is not reason enough to kill a boy. He asked the jurors to set aside their feelings and said it was not that the Crown wanted to convict anyone, but they were bound to "have regard for the facts." He told them it was not their job to be "moved by sympathy, compassion, or guilt."

But it was their job, if they wanted it to be. While they almost surely knew that Jackie was killed by his parents, they refused, as was their power as a jury, to convict.

Cruise later said that the Bateses had been proven guilty but had been "set free through the sympathy felt by everyone." A constable involved in the case said that the jury was "satisfied that the accused were legally guilty, but on account of the severity of the punishment refrained from bringing in a verdict to that effect." One juror apparently indicated as much. Another constable said that the jury was looking for a way to find the Bateses not guilty and the suggestion of the unlikely thymus death gave them one. If not that, Ludgate would have given them something else.

Ted and Rose were immediately set free and went on, as far as we can tell, to lead uneventful lives. Records are sketchy but they apparently separated for a while, Ted working as a butcher in Rosetown and Rose, oddly, living in Glidden. Eventually she came to live with Ted in Rosetown. Ted died there in 1954, at the age of 64. Rose returned to England where she died in 1978 in her mid-eighties.

Who could really quarrel with a verdict that spared these poor desperate people from the gallows? Ludgate was right when he warned the jury members that a verdict of guilty, and subsequent hangings, would be difficult for them to live with.

Did sparing Ted and Rose Bates harm the world in any way? Did it encourage other parents to kill their children? These two people suffered an unspeakable trauma and had to live out their lives with the horror of what they had done. The law said that we should kill them as well. The only barrier to this was the jury. The members of that jury in effect said no, we will not punish them further — we will not hang these people.

EMMETT TILL — MISSISSIPPI, 1955

Emmett Till was born in Chicago in 1941 and was killed in 1955. I was a bit surprised when I realized that he was just about my age. His murder seems so long ago, but had he survived an ill-fated trip to Mississippi in 1955, he would probably be alive today.

Although he had lost his father when he was four, he had a loving mother, and they led a happy life in Emmett's grandmother's house near downtown Chicago. Emmett survived polio although it left him with a bit of a stutter. Still he was an outgoing and lively boy, with lots of friends.

On August 20, 1955, Emmett's mother put him on a train headed south to visit relatives in the town of Money in northern Mississippi. He spent his first few days there visiting his cousins and then on the evening of August 24 went into town with some friends and relatives. They stopped at Bryant's Grocery and Meat Market in Money. Emmett followed one of the other boys into the store and stayed on briefly, after the other boy left. Working the cash register at the counter was a young white woman, Carolyn Bryant.

As one of Emmett's cousins later wrote, he joined Emmett in the store less than a minute later and saw nothing untoward as Emmett paid for a few things he had picked up; the two boys then left. Yet at the trial of the murderers Bryant claimed that Emmett had asked her for a date and had grabbed her by the waist, making suggestive comments.

Once outside, though, Emmett did make a fatal mistake. Bryant came out of the store and Emmett whistled at her, something that would probably have been barely noticed in the urban environment of Chicago. But he wasn't in Chicago anymore. Emmett's cousins knew immediately that he had crossed the line and had committed a socially unacceptable act. Black men were not allowed to make any sign that they found a white woman attractive. Emmett, of course, was just a boy, but it did not matter.

All of them, friends and family, were in real danger now. They quickly went back to their car and sped out of town. Over the next few days there was much talk in town about what had happened: a black boy whistling at a white woman. Bryant's husband, Roy, was very angry and felt that he had to do something. White townspeople generally felt that the boy had to be taught a lesson.

Roy Bryant and his half-brother John Milam went off in a pickup truck, looking for Emmett. They were accompanied, at first, by Carolyn Bryant and Johnny Washington, a black man who worked for Bryant. After grabbing the wrong boy and injuring him in the process, the vigilante posse carried on and eventually, at 2:30 a.m., found where Emmett was staying and pulled him out of bed and into the truck. There is some dispute over what exactly happened during the next few hours, but at some point the boy was shot and in the early morning his badly beaten body was dumped into the Tallahatchie River.

The body was returned to Chicago where, at his grieving mother's insistence, he was placed in an open casket in a funeral home. She wanted people to see "what had been done to her son." About 50,000 people filed by the casket. Chicago Mayor Richard Daly added his voice to the outraged calls for federal action against the murderers.

Within a day of the murder Bryant and Milam were arrested. About a week after the murder, a grand jury in Tallahatchie County in Mississippi indicted the two on murder and kidnapping charges. But trouble in seeking justice started almost immediately. The county sheriff, H.C. Strider, publicly proclaimed the body found was likely not that of Emmett Till. Strider said it was more like the body of a man and it looked like it had been in the water too long to be Emmett Till. Of course the body had already been identified by the friends he had been staying with and later by his mother. And he was still wearing a ring left to him by his father.

Jury selection started on September 19, but no black residents of Tallahatchie County were eligible — you had to be a registered voter and none were. The defence team, assisted by the sheriff, ensured that all the white men chosen were "safe" ones: there was no chance they would find Bryant and Milam guilty.

There was no doubt that Bryant and Milam had abducted Emmett and virtually no doubt that they had been involved in his killing. The defence presented a pretext for finding the two not guilty; but any pretext probably would have worked. Sheriff Strider repeated his ridiculous and contested theory that the body was not the body of Emmett Till at all. The prosecutor made an impassioned plea for justice, but the defence attorneys trumped that by telling the jurors, "every last Anglo-Saxon one of you has the courage to set these men free."

And so they did.

Bryant and Milam subsequently fell on hard times as the shops they operated were boycotted by blacks, and blacks refused to work on their farms. The two murderers lost their businesses and turned to bootlegging. They admitted the abduction and murder in a story sold to *Look* magazine in 1956, for a fee of $3,500. Milam died in 1980 and Bryant lived on until 1994.

* * *

This was indeed a terrible use of jury nullification, and it is frequently cited by those who oppose jury independence and nullification. One can see why.

Is this threat of racism sufficient reason to suppress or even abolish these ideas? Perhaps. This problem of racism is examined in detail in Chapter 8.

There was one good outcome to this sorry incident: the horror of this lynching and subsequent shambles of a trial outraged the nation and led to large protest rallies in many cities. It signalled the beginning of the civil rights movement that changed the character of the nation. Later that same year Rosa Parks, a great hero of the civil rights movement, cited the Till case as a reason for her activism.

KAWAS NANAVATI – INDIA, 1959

Kawas Nanavati, his beautiful, English-born wife, Sylvia, and their three children moved in secrecy to Toronto some time after his release from prison in India in the mid-1960s. It is unlikely that his friends and neighbours in his new country knew that he had been the central figure in a sensational crime and trial, with drastic consequences for the Indian justice system. Little is known about their lives in Canada, except that Kawas died in 2003. Sylvia may still be alive.

Kawas and Sylvia met in Portsmouth, England, in 1949 when she was eighteen and he was twenty-four and a Commander in the Indian Navy. He proposed within a month; they married and moved to Bombay.

Kawas was a highly decorated officer with very powerful connections. He was known as an upright officer with strong sense of honour. Sylvia apparently enjoyed her life with her husband and participating in high society in Bombay.

But trouble lay ahead. Kawas's close friend of fifteen years, Prem Ahuja, was a handsome and gregarious man with a reputation as a play-boy. Sylvia had become lonely during her husband's many absences for his work, and Prem began to visit her while Kawas was away. Apparently Kawas knew of these meetings and approved of them, thinking his friend was just helping out. But before long the relationship progressed beyond a friendship. In a letter to Prem on March 19, 1958, Sylvia wrote, "Nothing else is as important as my being with you."

Apparently Sylvia took the relationship much more seriously than Prem did. Although he had talked of marriage in the early stages of the relationship, he avoided the subject later. Sylvia, for her part, was quite ready to leave her family, divorce Kawas, and marry Prem. But at some point Prem lost interest in this idea and apparently tried to make it clear to her, talking to her about other women he might marry.

On April 27, 1959, shortly after he had returned home from a trip, Kawas had planned to take his family to a movie, but Sylvia was distracted and aloof. Kawas tried to find out what was wrong and after a time she told him she had been having an affair with Prem. Kawas was stunned, then said he had to go and see Prem. She warned him that Prem might shoot him, but Kawas indicated that he was going to shoot himself anyway. She cried out no, why should he shoot himself, he was the innocent one.

Kawas took Sylvia and the children to the movie but did not go in himself. Instead he went to find Prem. At trial Sylvia was asked why she let her husband go off in an agitated state when he might kill himself or be killed. She said she was upset and not thinking clearly and "It is difficult to explain these things to children, so I took them to the cinema."

It was a disastrous decision. Apparently still infatuated with Prem, Sylvia perhaps, at that moment, did not care what happened to Kawas. Just ten days earlier she had written to Prem, "nothing is going to stop my coming to you. My decision is made and I don't change my mind."

But her mind was changed for her. Kawas took a pistol to Prem's flat, found him emerging from a bath wearing only a towel, and shot him three times, killing him. According to Kawas, he had first demanded to know if Prem was going to marry Sylvia and accept their children. Kawas claimed that Prem had answered, "Will I marry every woman I sleep with?" This inflamed Kawas, he testified, and in an ensuing struggle with the gun he claimed he accidentally shot Prem.

The prosecution, however, had a strong counter-case. Why had Prem's towel not come undone during the struggle? Why had three shots been fired? Why had the whole encounter been so quick, as a servant testified? Why had Kawas not explained to Prem's sister, who was in the house, that it had been an accident? Why had Kawas — a man supposedly in shock and not really knowing what he was doing — been so composed and deliberate throughout the whole episode, calmly finding a gun at the naval base and then, after the killing, calmly unloading the gun and turning himself in?

Was Prem's murder something that happened in the heat of the moment or was it premeditated? The prosecution had a very strong case for the latter, but the people were for Kawas Nanavati. The jury found him not guilty, by a margin of eight to one. This was later overturned in a higher court, and Nanavati was given a life sentence. After complex legal manoeuvring, Nanavati was released after three years in prison. Throughout the proceedings and jail term Sylvia stood by him. And then they secretly went off to a new life in Toronto.

* * *

A number of Indian films were made of Nanavati's story, and various accounts of it were written. Salman Rushdie's novel *Midnight's Children* has a chapter called "Commander Sabarmati's Baton," which is a fiction-alized account of the story.

* * *

The debate over jury nullification has been settled in India. The Indian government was so outraged by what it perceived as the influence of public opinion on the jury's verdict in the Nanavati trial that it abolished trial by jury in India. Jury nullification could never again happen there. There would be no juries at all!

GRANT KRIEGER – ALBERTA, 2003

In 1978, twenty-four-year-old Grant Krieger, who lived in Regina at the time, was diagnosed with multiple sclerosis. Krieger had married a few years before and he and his wife had recently had their first child. The diagnosis was a terrible blow to him, as it would be for any person.

Various pain-killers were prescribed for Krieger, but nothing seemed to work very well, and after years of frustration he became depressed and in 1994 attempted suicide. Then a friend suggested he try marijuana, which he did, and it seemed to be the one treatment that worked well for him. He initially obtained his drug on the black market, but feared getting caught.

He and his wife became advocates for the legalization of marijuana.

In 2000, Krieger was given a judicial exemption to grow and use the drug for his own medical purposes. However, he encountered many others who could benefit from the drug, as he had, so he began to supply them as well. He did this openly and vowed not to stop, even if he got into trouble over it.

In 2001 he was charged with trafficking in marijuana after police found twenty-nine plants in his home in Bowness, Alberta. He admitted selling the drug to those with AIDS, epilepsy, and other diseases. In a clear case of nullification, his jury of eleven women and one man found him not guilty. Krieger was tried again on the same charges in 2003, and this is where the story gets really interesting.

This trial was presided over by Justice Paul Chrumka, who was undoubtedly aware that jury nullification had decided the 2001 trial. He apparently was not about to have that happen in his court. As in the first trial there was no doubt that Krieger had committed the offence, and Chrumka wanted to be sure that the jury, this time, came to the "right" verdict. At the end of the proceedings, in his final instructions to the jury, he told them:

> . . . to retire to the jury room to consider what I have said, appoint one of yourselves to be your foreperson, and then return to the court with a verdict of guilty.

This was an extraordinary thing to do. What was the jury there for, if only to be told what verdict to reach? Why waste time having a jury at all?

Chrumka, however, was not about to back down. When some jurors questioned his instruction he said to the full group:

> I have a matter that the jury raises. It is apparent that some of the members either didn't understand my direction this morning, that

is that they were to return a verdict of guilty . . . or they refused to do so. . . it's up to them to bring it in [the verdict of guilty] — to abide by the direction.

When a juror complained about how it was difficult having only two choices, guilty or not guilty, Chrumka said:

Actually there is one choice, and that is guilt.

The jury did what it understood from Chrumka's unequivocal instructions: they found Krieger guilty. But then the story gets even more extraordinary.

Krieger's lawyers, of course, appealed the verdict, on the grounds that a judge cannot direct a verdict of guilty. A judge *can* in effect direct a verdict of not guilty by dismissing a case on the grounds of insufficient evidence, but a judge, in a jury trial, cannot find the accused guilty. One would think this would be obvious to everyone: clearly, if judges could determine guilt, juries would have no purpose.

How could Chrumka, a man well-versed in the law, think he could get away with such a huge and obvious legal mistake and then reiterate it a number of times, proving that it was not just a slip of the tongue. How could this happen? Who knows? Surely the appeal court would correct this travesty.

In a judgment more astonishing than Chrumka's comments, the Appeal Court of Alberta denied Krieger's appeal of his conviction by a vote of two to one! I needed to look in some detail at that judgment. Was I missing something in all of this?

The three who heard the appeal were Alberta Chief Justice Catherine Fraser, Mr. Justice Jean Côté, and Madam Justice Ellen Picard. The majority opinion was held by the latter two. The essence of their argument was that the trial judge may have erred in directing a verdict of guilty, but that does not warrant a new trial because:

1) the only possible value to the accused would be jury nullification, because the accused is clearly guilty;

2) granting a new trial is premised on having a jury act reasonably;

3) it is clear that a reasonable jury would not nullify and would find a verdict of guilty; and, therefore,

4) there is no point in a new trial.

The two justices added a comment that if jurors did nullify it would be to ignore a new trial judge's instructions and "to ignore their oaths," the sworn statement they must make when they are accepted as a juror. So here we have an image of jury nullification as something practiced only by unreasonable men and women who are untrue to their oaths.

And here was open and direct denial of jury independence by not only Chrumka, but Côté and Picard as well. With the actions of these three justices, we see an attempt to nullify jury nullification and to quash the idea of jury independence. Did they have the right to do this? It is one thing to try to encourage jurors to follow the law — I am with those who support that. It is another to stand in the way of the long-accepted notion of jury independence and to block nullification. These three justices were in effect trying to change a legal tradition that has existed in English law for 340 years (as you will see in Chapter 3).

Alberta Chief Justice Catherine Fraser, the third member of the Appeal Court, wrote an eloquent and persuasive dissenting opinion. She summarizes arguments against nullification but states that it is a power of juries that no judge has the right to deny. Her thoughtful opinion goes on for about six pages; her dismissive colleagues' rejection of the appeal occurs in five short paragraphs. The whole judgment has the feel of an adult, Fraser, dealing with two recalcitrant children, Côté and Picard, all of whom have equal votes.

Fortunately, this was not the end of the story; public outrage greeted the Appeal Court's decision and many legal observers recognized that the conviction could not possibly stand. The appeal went to the Supreme Court of Canada, where reason finally took over. In 2006 the court reviewed Chrumka's actions and the Alberta Appeal Court's decision and then decisively ruled in Krieger's favour. Justice Fish wrote a stinging and unusually blunt rebuke to Chrumka and the Alberta Appeal judges Côté and Picard:

> [Alberta Chief Justice Catherine Fraser] would have allowed the appeal, quashed the conviction and ordered a new trial. So, too, would I.

Fish's commentary is a joy to read. He went on to write:

> [Chrumka] evidently considered it his duty to order the jury to convict and to make it plain to the jurors that they were not free to reach any other conclusion . . . in effect, the trial judge reduced the jury's role to a ceremonial one: he ordered the conviction and left the jury, as a matter of form but not of substance, its delivery in open court.

Fish pointed out that Chrumka was in violation of the *Charter of Rights*:

> . . . the trial judge unfortunately deprived the jurors of the responsibility that was by law theirs alone. [Krieger] was thereby deprived of his constitutional right "to the benefit of trial by jury."

Fish conjured up the image of William Penn and his jury from 340 years ago, when the right of jury independence was first established (see Chapter 3). He compared Chrumka to the presiding senior judge in Penn's case, the Lord Mayor of London:

In another era, the usual enticement to quick agreement [to a guilty verdict] consisted of locking the jury up without "meat, drink, fire and tobacco." Jurors who gave verdicts thought unacceptable by the court were punished . . . fined and imprisoned for their verdict of "not guilty."

Some called the ruling in this case the most expected decision in the history of the Supreme Court of Canada. The verdict against Krieger case was quashed, and this rebellion by the triumvirate of Chrumka, Côté and Picard, against a cornerstone of our legal system, was also quashed.

* * *

In Krieger's first trial he was found not guilty by a jury that refused to follow the law; this is not an uncommon response in trials for marijuana offences. Similar refusals to convict were common for those caught drinking in the Prohibition Era. Jury nullification comes into play whenever laws are lagging behind community standards. That is the case now for minor drug offences, just as it was for violations of prohibition in the United States in the 1920s and early '30s.

In such cases we can see jury nullification as a vehicle for social reform, as it was in the Zenger case.

In Krieger's second trial Chrumka tried to circumvent the will of the jury, but ultimately succeeded only in proving the inconsistency and illogicality of a jury system in which verdicts of guilty could be directed by the presiding judge.

* * *

Out of curiosity I checked into what has happened to the major players in the odd Krieger drama.

In 2007 Krieger was tried again and this time, with a less forgiving jury, given a four-month sentence for drug trafficking. He avoided jail by signing, in March 2009, a legal document pledging to stop growing or distributing marijuana. "I'm at the end of all my ropes," he said. "I'm just tired of it now." He was fifty-four years old at the time. He had been fighting prosecution for thirteen years and had lost his family, lost his driver's license, and gone heavily into debt. He still needed the drug for his medical condition, but planned to get it on the black market "like everyone else."

As of early 2013, Justices Fraser, Côté, and Picard still sit on the Alberta Court of Appeals. Fraser is still the Chief Justice of Alberta and received an honourary doctorate from the University of Calgary in 2007. Côté has been author of a number of controversial decisions. Previously, in 1992, Picard had received an honourary doctorate from the University of Alberta.

In 2009 Chrumka was honoured by the Law Society of Alberta for 50 years of service. He obtained his law degree from the University of Alberta in 1958 and became a judge in 1982, serving in Alberta the Yukon and the Northwest Territories, retiring in 2007. In 2010 Chrumka was appointed for a two-year term with the Alberta Human Rights Commission. He was the recipient of the Alberta Centennial Medal and the Queen Elizabeth II Golden Jubilee Medal, both of which, according to the biography on the Human Rights Commission website, "recognize outstanding and exemplary contributions to society."

PRITCHARD AND OLDITCH – UK, 2007

Phil Pritchard and Toby Olditch were two self-employed carpenters living in Oxford, England. Neither was a pacifist and neither seemed a likely candidate to become a war protestor, but in the early 2000s the two men, then in their early thirties, pledged to do whatever they could to stop Britain from participating in what the two viewed as unjust wars. They were both upset about British plans to join the invasion of Iraq, and on the night of March 18, 2003, the night before Britain was to start its bombing of Baghdad, the two men decided to act.

They drove to the Gloucestershire air force base, known as Royal Air Force Station Fairford. The station was used mainly as a standby airfield and had not been in everyday use but at the time was being used by American B-52 bombers preparing for the upcoming attack on Iraq. The airfield had become the focus of British protests against the Iraq war.

Five days earlier, Margaret Jones, a fifty-seven-year-old university lecturer from Bristol, and Paul Milling, sixty-one, a former York magistrate and councillor, had broken into the same airfield. Using hammers and bolt cutters they damaged fuel tankers and wagons used for carrying bombs. The cost of repairing the damage was about $20,000. Jones, Milling, Pritchard, Olditch, and a fifth conspirator, Josh Richards, came to be known as the "Fairford Five."

Pritchard and Olditch were not exactly skilled operatives, however — perhaps a little more like Inspector Clouseau than James Bond. They were weighed down with too much gear: bolts to be placed in the engines of the B-52s, bolt cutters to get through the fencing, pictures of happy Iraqi to attach to the aircraft doors, paint to daub on the aircraft, cameras to photograph what they had done, and even supplies like toothbrushes they would use when sent to jail. They wore flashing headbands in the hope that no one would shoot them. The trouble with that idea was that someone would see them.

Still, the intrepid pair, who came to be known as the "B-52 Two," managed to cut through an outer fence and slip under a layer of razor wire and cross the field toward the runway where the bombers were resting. Unfortunately for them, the field was full of nettles. One can imagine Clouseau in such a situation.

They never actually made it to the runway, although they got close. They were caught by patrolling police officers, probably attracted by the flashing headbands, and taken to jail. Records do not show if they were allowed to keep their toothbrushes. Pritchard later said that during the arrest he kept thinking about what an ass he was. No planes were prevented from taking off to bomb Iraq. The two men were charged with conspiracy to commit criminal damage.

The hapless young men first went to trial in October 2006, a trial which resulted in a hung jury (a jury that could not agree on a verdict). A second trial was held in May 2007 in the city of Bristol, a little over an hour's drive from Fairford. Pritchard said he hoped they would be acquitted but was prepared for something like a five-year sentence — presumably he had his toothbrush then.

Their defence was they were trying to prevent war crimes — specifically the use of cluster bombs. They said it was necessary because other tactics — protests — had failed. British law states, "a person may use such force as reasonable in the prevention of a crime." These two were just trying to do what they could to prevent a crime — the war crime of an unlawful attack on Iraq.

The jury in the Bristol courtroom found the B-52 Two not guilty. Defence lawyer Mike Schwartz claimed that the jury was saying that war crimes had been committed. But it seems likely that the jury's reasons were not so simple as that.

When Margaret Jones and Paul Milling were tried in the same courtroom a few months later, using the same defence, they were found guilty. But Josh Richards, the fifth conspirator, was treated like Pritchard and Olditch and he survived two trials without a conviction. Why the different treatment for Jones and Milling?

The main difference in the Jones and Milling case was that they had caused actual damage, while Pritchard, Olditch, and Richards had not. Technically that would not matter; all had been involved in a conspiracy to do damage, and getting caught before actually doing damage does not erase the liability. But to the juries apparently it did matter.

It seems likely that most or all of the jury members were sympathetic to the protestors' view of the war but that their sympathies drew the line at property damage. Finding Jones and Milling guilty suggested that, when actual damage was done, the defence of preventing war crimes was not accepted.

But because Prichard, Olditch and Richards had done no real harm, and even though they were technically just as guilty as Jones and Milling, their juries refused to convict them. This probably was a case of juries willing to nullify, so long as the damage done was not too great. Or maybe they just could not convict two such comically inept protestors.

CHAPTER 3

HOW IT ALL BEGAN: JAILING JURORS

William Penn (1644–1718) was, to put it mildly, a somewhat difficult and stubborn man. But he was also a brilliant one and an influential writer and speaker. His father, Admiral Penn, found favour in the Court of Charles II and was knighted and made Commander of the Navy. The Admiral's son had a mind of his own, however, and a strong sense of conscience, and he was never comfortable with the aristocratic life of his parents. From a young age he seemed to be seeking something he felt was more high-minded and principled. Although never a Puritan, he affected many practices of the Puritans and, especially later in life, was known for his "serious demeanor, strict behavior and lack of humour."

Sent to Oxford at the age of sixteen, with an assigned servant and the status of a "gentleman scholar," William became troubled by the attitude he found there toward religious dissent. His fellow aristocratic Anglicans harassed and persecuted students of other faiths, particularly Quakers. Penn found this distasteful and sided with the Quakers, whom he had learned about a year earlier when Quaker missionary Thomas Loe had been a houseguest of the Penns.

William's attraction to the now-disfavoured Quakers at Oxford caused great distress to his parents, who felt he was going to squander his career possibilities at Court. But William was more concerned about principles than prospects. Dean Owen of the University was fired for excessive "free-thinking" and Penn stood by him, causing the university to fine and reprimand him. Later Penn protested the university's requirement to go to the Anglican chapel services as "forced worship," a good point but one that found little favour in the university hierarchy, and he was expelled.

The Admiral was apoplectic. He beat his son and forced him from their home, although William's mother eventually negotiated a peace settlement and had him return. But the senior Penns were both worried about how William's exploits might affect their own social status. They sent him to Europe for two years.

William returned in 1664 to help manage the family's affairs while his father went back to sea. By this time William had become an impressive figure of a man, well-dressed, handsome, and well-spoken. He even seemed to have loosened up a little. He remained, though, a man of high principle. In Paris he had been attacked by a man with a sword over some alleged affront. Penn with his own sword subdued the man without hurting him and then released him. Of the event Penn wrote:

I ask any man of understanding or conscience if the whole round of ceremony were worth the life of a man.

While tending to business at his family's home, Penn continued to find himself drawn to the Quakers. During an outbreak of the plague, he admired the good work done by the Quakers in helping the sick. He loved the honesty and the principled nature of the Society of Friends; it suited his own character and predilections. He became a regular attendee at the Quaker meeting house.

As the regime of Charles II became more aggressive toward non-

Anglican religious activities, it became dangerous to participate in Quaker meetings. But Penn was not deterred. In 1667 he was arrested for attending a Quaker meeting, but because of his aristocratic attire the police offered to let him go. He refused. Instead, he wrote to the authorities responsible for the arrest in a letter that was his first expression of "the noble principle in behalf of universal toleration." He had found a cause: religious freedom.

Penn's parents were most distressed that he had "become Quaker" and implored him to accept the high station of wealth and honour to which he was entitled, but he chose the much riskier company of the Friends. As one biographer wrote of Penn, "he was willing to bear the reproaches of society which in that era were everywhere cast upon them [the Quakers]."

The elder Penns, though, saw his actions not as principled but as madness. The Admiral tried everything he could think of to dissuade his son from associating with the despised and persecuted Quakers. In frustration and despair he asked his son if he would at least take off his hat in the company of the King and senior members of the Court. This was a matter of deep conviction on the part of Quakers, for whom anything in the nature of a religious duty, even the doffing of a hat, was not unimportant. They felt that uncovering the head was an act of reverence to be reserved for God, not for mortal beings. Out of respect for his father, Penn agreed to consider his request, which he did briefly, but then, to his father's continued distress, reiterated his belief and his stance.

This matter of the hats enraged officials in courts and only increased the punishment inflicted on Quakers. But to Penn and the Friends this was a symbolic matter: were they entitled to their beliefs or were they not? The Quakers would not use the common phrase "your humble servant," which they felt was only an expression of human pride and connoted no real humility or reverence. Quakers also refused to swear oaths in court, on the grounds that Jesus had spoken against swearing. Eventually, due to the Quakers' constancy in regard to these matters, the courts relented on some of them.

Despite his father's pleading, Penn simply insisted that these basic principles could not be compromised, "for once begun, there remains no place to take a stand." His distraught father again threw his son out of his house and Penn lived for years in relative poverty, depending on help from other Quakers to survive. He could have been a highly favoured member of the royal court; instead he was cast out by his father, attached to a despised religious sect, and scorned by his former friends.

At the urging of Penn's mother, the Admiral, perhaps sensing that his son was a man of unusual character, began to relent somewhat and allowed him food and shelter, if not openly countenancing him.

Penn became a religious writer and preacher who went to jail many times for his supposedly heretical views, none of which threatened the state in any way (as opposed to views of the Puritans, who would have imposed their ideas on the state) but all of which simply sought basic religious freedoms. Penn argued that Quakers ought to be allowed to worship according to the ideas they held dear, not that everyone else must hold to the same ideas.

The emergence of William Penn as a man of great personal integrity, devoted to the organization that best reflected the values and principles he most admired, set the stage for his famous trial. He was to be at the centre of events that not only resulted in a tour guide's admiring comments 340 years later, and a laudatory embroidery still hung inside the lobby of a London hotel, but in establishing a fundamental principle of English law, a principle that continues on today in most countries with legal systems based upon English law.

Penn of course went on to fame in the New World, managing a huge tract of land later to be called Pennsylvania, but his stand in 1670, and the response evoked in his jury, undoubtedly rank as the most influential events of his life.

* * *

Juries of peers are usually dated from 1215 and the signing of Magna Carta, but some versions can be traced back to much earlier times. The idea is that justice is best served with judgment rendered by a group of disinterested peers — equals who have no vested interest in the outcome. Presumably such people are free to seek true justice, unencumbered by the biases or self-interest of either individuals or the state.

King John, the central figure in this part of the story, and William Penn, the main player in the other part, were probably as different as two men could be. Whereas Penn was driven by a powerful moral sensibility — he would do what his conscience told him regardless of the consequences — John was a pragmatist who would do anything to further his own prospects. Both of these men had a profound effect on British law, Penn through his intellect, eloquence, and determined honesty, John by so abusing his powers as King that he brought about a rebellion that forced his acceptance of Magna Carta, establishing for the first time that the King, like other people, was not above the law.

In 1199 John succeeded his brother Richard the Lionheart who, though a successful warrior, spent little time in Britain. John was said to be more attentive to the business of the realm, but became engaged in a number of expensive battles to keep the European lands won by his predecessors. Employing a large army of mercenaries, John found himself desperate to raise money, a problem that grew worse with each territory he lost, each of them having previously been a source of revenue.

John used an acute business sense to wring every possible bit of money out of every possible source. He ignored customs and traditions in order to extort money from everyone from the rural peasants to various levels of nobles to the tenant-in-chief. He devised many different schemes for raising money, including ensuring favourable judgments in legal proceedings in return for large sums of money. He exploited and expanded the practice of seeking payment from feudal tenants in order to avoid military service. He became increasingly unscrupulous and punitive in collecting on debts. He seized land, took hostages, and imprisoned defaulters.

John had to increase the revenue from the barons — the great landowners and warlords of the realm — to pay for his military undertakings. The barons became increasingly resentful, and they began to organize against the King. After an unsuccessful assassination attempt in 1212 a group of dissident barons pressed for reform.

At a famous rendezvous in a meadow called Runnymede in the spring of 1215, an agreement for reform, called the Articles of the Barons, was hammered out. Whether or not the King was present is uncertain, but in any case, the agreement was made between the barons and representatives of the King, if not the King himself. The document contained forty-nine articles setting out unprecedented concessions by the King. Soon afterwards the agreement was expanded to sixty-three articles, in what was then called the Great Charter: Magna Carta.

Although viewed as such centuries later, the Great Charter was not initially seen as a document citing fundamental principles of liberty. Instead it was a document to appease the barons for long-standing grievances in regard to arbitrary actions of kings. John himself apparently had no intention of ruling according to the provisions of the document. He almost immediately used an appeal to the Pope to get it annulled, which did happen a few months later, only for it to be reinstated a year later, after John died.

The concessions in the document were indeed unprecedented. This was the first agreement that the king, like other citizens of the realm, would be constrained by law. John probably thought the idea would disappear with annulment of the charter, but the idea was so powerful that once articulated it would not die with a pope's decree. The idea eventually became a cornerstone of English law and all legal systems based on it: equal justice under the law.

Most of the articles of Magna Carta dealt with feudal administration and taxation and are now obsolete. These did not abolish John's rights, but regulated them, thus (in theory) preventing the arbitrary fundraising undertaken by the king in the past.

Two clauses, however, are enduring:

> *39. No free man shall be seized or imprisoned or stripped of his rights or possessions, or outlawed or exiled, or deprived of his standing in any other way, nor will we proceed with force against him, or send others to do so, except by the lawful judgment of his equals or by the law of the land.*

> *40. To no one will we sell, to no one deny or delay right or justice.*

These clauses had their origins in the desire to curb King John's use of the justice system as a source of private revenue, but the importance of the words as expressing fundamental ideas of justice have only strengthened over the generations since.

In 1225, Magna Carta was reissued under the seal of Henry III. It was reconfirmed by many late medieval kings and then in the seventeenth century was recognized by legal scholars and lawyers as containing statements concerning fundamental principles of law. Today, clauses thirty-nine and forty remain statements of fundamental human freedoms.

William Penn wrote a commentary on Magna Carta and used parts of it as the basis for laws in founding the State of Pennsylvania. Many other influential legal documents have drawn from it, including the American Declaration of Independence and the 1948 United Nations Universal Declaration of Human Rights.

* * *

But what does the phrase "except by the lawful judgment of his equals or by the law of the land" really mean? In the mid-fourteenth century the somewhat unclear phrase "lawful judgment of his equals" was rewritten as a right to trial by peers. Our modern idea of jury trials was established.

However, what about the clause immediately after "lawful judgment of his equals," where it says "or by the law of the land"? This seems to imply that the law could override the wishes of juries. This matter, concerning the very fundamental legal issue of the independence of juries, was unclear until the landmark trial of William Penn and his friend William Meade in 1670.

* * *

Penn had become a member of the Society of Friends in 1667 and distinguished himself as a lay minister and writer of religious works. But trouble was coming. In 1670 the British parliament passed the *Conventicle Act*, ostensibly to ban "seditious conventicles" — clandestine religious meetings aimed at overthrowing the state. Quaker meetings were in no way seditious, nor were they secret. The real purpose of the *Act* seems to have been to suppress all religious meetings conducted in any manner other than in accord with the liturgy of the Church of England.

The *Act* violated various ancient customs and principles of English law, including Magna Carta, by doing away with jury trials and authorizing justices of the peace to punish offenders. One clause read:

> . . . that in any case of reasonable doubt about the interpretation of it, the Act should be considered most largely and beneficially for the suppression of conventicles.

This was contrary to the long-standing legal principle that the defendant should have the advantage of doubt. The *Act* was clearly a device for religious repression and as such offended William Penn and his fellow Quakers. And, in practice, whether it was intended or not, Quakers became the main group affected by the *Act*. They refused to change the time and place of their meetings, holding that no human authority could prevent them from worshiping at a time and place they believed God had determined for them. Most other religious dissenters stayed out of sight, changing times and places so they could not easily be detected. Not so the Quakers, who thus became easy targets for prosecution.

Penn in particular was determined to defy what he considered to be an unjust act, regardless of the consequences. He went to a scheduled meeting outside a home on Gracechurch Street that was being watched by authorities. At the gathering, as is Quaker custom, all remained silent for a time, after which Penn started to speak. At that point, he and another member of the group, William Meade, were arrested and taken to a grim prison near Newgate Market. Since the charge involved holding a seditious conventicle, Penn and Meade could have been executed if found guilty.

The famous trial was held in London's criminal court, the Old Bailey, and was presided over by Samuel Starling, the Mayor of London, and nine other judges. The jury consisted of twelve men from London. As was the custom of the time (a practice that was probably responsible for a high conviction rate), Penn and Meade defended themselves. But Penn and Meade were no ordinary defendants. Penn in particular was eloquent and persuasive in his defence, so much so that the court eventually removed him from the immediate proceedings, placing first him, then Meade, in a closed corner of the room called the bale-dock, from which it was difficult to participate.

The trial was improper from the start, a travesty of justice that probably encouraged jurors to side with Penn and Meade. On the first day, in the morning of September 1, 1670, the indictment against the two men was read out — a lengthy one charging that the two men ". . . unlawfully and tumultuously did assemble and congregate themselves together to the disturbance of the peace . . ." There had indeed been some tumult, but it had been caused by the arrests, not by Penn talking to his congregation. Both men pleaded not guilty. Their case was set aside for five hours while other cases were heard, then the court adjourned to September 3.

As Penn and Meade were asked to approach the bar for the second time, the mayor noticed that their hats had been removed, probably snatched off by the clerk. Quakers, of course, felt that removing hats was something they did only for God, not for men. But now they were hatless. Speaking to the clerk, the mayor said:

Sirrah, who bid you put off their hats? Put on their hats again.

Whereupon an officer did so. The mayor understood that the two Quakers would not then voluntarily remove their hats.

Court (speaking now to the defendants): *Do you know where you are?*

Penn: *Yes*

Court: *Do you not know it is the king's court?*

Penn: *I know it to be a court, and I suppose it to be the king's court.*

Court: *Do you not know there is respect due to the court?*

Penn: *Yes.*

Court: *Why do you not pay it then?*

Penn: *I do so.*

Court: *Why do you not pull off your hat then?*

Penn: *Because I do not believe that to be any respect.*

Court: *Well, the court sets forty marks apiece upon your heads, as a fine for your contempt of court.*

Penn: *I desire it might be observed that we came into court with our hats off . . . and if they have been put on since it was by order from the bench, and therefore not we, but the bench, should be fined.*

Such was the manifest unfairness of the trial, a stark contrast between a punitive and arbitrary court and an eloquent and appealing defendant. It would not have been uncommon for a court at that time to act arbitrarily and unfairly, but here it had to win its case against a very strong-willed, well-educated, and articulate individual.

Penn and Meade went on to challenge the court's application of the law, which is when they were placed in the bale-dock. The prosecution proceeded in an arbitrary and high-handed manner, with occasional attempts at interventions from Penn and Meade, shouting from the bale-dock. The case was completed in a short time, with no real defence being allowed. Meade's last words, heard from the bale-dock, were:

I say these are barbarous and unjust proceedings.

The two men were held in a cell to wait until coming back to hear their fate, which the mayor and other judges were certain would be to be declared guilty and then, possibly, hanged. How could it be otherwise? The men had broken the law, such as it was. The jury was sent out to reach its expected verdict of guilty.

The judges, soon realizing that there were at least some jurors not inclined to find Penn and Meade guilty, berated them with very menacing language. After some time the jury did return with its verdict. The clerk asked "is William Penn guilty of the matter whereof he stands indicted in manner and form, or not guilty?"

The jury foreman replied, "Guilty of speaking in Gracechurch Street." The court demanded to know if that was all, and the foreman said it was. The court said the verdict was as good as nothing without reference to it being an unlawful assembly — that the accused were guilty of speaking to an unlawful assembly. As it was, it was equivalent to a not guilty verdict.

The court was outraged and in turn vilified and threatened the jury. One judge said "the law of England will not allow you to part until you have given your verdict."

"We have given our verdict," the jury foreman replied. "We can give no other."

The jury was sent out briefly and came back again with essentially the same verdict, Penn was guilty of preaching to an assembly, and added that Meade was not guilty of anything, even of speaking in Gracechurch Street. They refused to add that it was an unlawful assembly.

This time an observer reported that "this [verdict] both the mayor and recorder resented at so high a rate, that they exceeded the bounds of all reason and civility." They particularly blamed one juror, Edward Bushel, whom they thought to be a Quaker sympathizer. "Will you be led by such a silly fellow?" the Mayor asked. "An impudent, cunning fellow?" The jury was told it would not be dismissed until it brought in a verdict the court could accept.

The absurdity of having the court require a particular verdict must have been dawning on some of these judges. Why have a jury at all if it is not free to come a decision different from that desired by the court? Penn, who along with Meade had been brought back into hear the verdict, weighed in on this point:

My jury, who are my judges, ought not to be menaced; their verdict should be free and not compelled; the bench ought to wait upon them, but not forestall them. I do desire that justice may be done me, and that the arbitrary resolves of the bench may not be the measure of my jury's verdict.

"Stop that prating fellow's mouth," a court official said, "or put him out of court." But Penn went on:

> The agreement of twelve men is a verdict in law, and such a one being given by the jury, I require the clerk of the peace to record it, as he will answer it at his peril.

The jurors reiterated their determination to stand by their verdict; the court responded by ordering the jury to be kept all night without meat, drink, fire, or even a chamber pot.

At 7:00 a.m. the next morning (September 4) the prisoners were brought back and the jury was called in again. The verdict? "William Penn is guilty of speaking in Gracechurch Street." This was repeated once again, with the jury again being threatened by the court. Penn spoke again:

> It is intolerable that my jury should be thus menaced: is this according to the fundamental laws? Are they not my proper judges by the great Charter of England? What hope is there of ever having justice done, when juries are threatened, and their verdicts rejected? I am concerned to speak and grieved to see such arbitrary proceedings . . . Unhappy are those juries who are threatened to be fined, and starved, and ruined, if they give not in verdicts contrary to their consciences.

The Mayor replied with, "Stop his mouth; gaoler, bring fetters and stake him to the ground."

"Do your pleasure," Penn replied. "I matter not your fetters."

After more threats and references to the methods of the Spanish Inquisition, and assurances that a new law would be passed requiring juries to follow the law, the jury was sent out again, under protest, returning again at 7:00 a.m. the next morning.

This time the jury, fed up with the treatment they had been receiving, minced no words. "Not guilty," they said.

The court then fined them 40 marks per man, the equivalent of a year's wages, and imprisoned them until the debt was paid. Penn assumed he and Meade would be set free but they too were sent back to prison, for having worn their hats in court.

One man, the aforementioned Edward Bushel, refused to pay the fine. Instead he petitioned the Court of Common Pleas for a writ of *habeas corpus*, which was eventually granted and he was released. Sir John Vaughan, Chief Justice of the Court of Common Pleas, then ruled that a jury could not be punished for the verdict it returned, thus establishing jury independence.

* * *

William Penn's evident sense of honour and decency inspired his jurors to refuse to be bullied by the court and to stand up for what was right. The resulting power of jury independence has remained a basic principle of English law and of most countries following English law. It has been a factor in many trials, in both good and not so good ways, throughout the past 340 years, as we saw in the examples in Chapter 2.

We can admire Penn and his jurors, but what are we to think today of this principle of jury independence and the power of juries to nullify the law? If we look at the case of John Peter Zenger, and how it led to establishment of the principle of freedom of speech in the United States, we might think it to be a very good thing indeed. If we look at murderers escaping punishment, as in the Donnelly massacre and the murder of Emmett Till, we might have our doubts.

What can we make of this? Read on!

CHAPTER 4

MORGENTALER: NOT GUILTY

No jury would ever convict me.

Henry Morgentaler

An unlikely hero to millions of Canadians, and a villain to some others, Henry Morgentaler was born in Lodz, Poland in 1923. When the Nazis occupied Poland, Henry, his brother Abraham, and their parents were confined to a ghetto in Lodz. His father, Josef, a Jewish social activist, was arrested and killed by the Gestapo. The two boys and their mother, Golda, lived on in the ghetto until 1944, when the Germans forced the ghetto inhabitants into concentration camps. The three surviving Morgentalers, along with another Jewish family, the Rosenfarbs, hid out for two days but were then discovered and sent to Auschwitz. Golda died there; the boys were sent on to Dachau. When they were liberated by the US Army on April 29, 1945, the twenty-two-year-old Henry weighed just seventy pounds.

After the war both boys eventually made their way to North America, Abraham to the United States in 1946 and Henry to Montreal in

1950. In 1949, while still in Europe, Henry had married his girlfriend from Lodz, Chavea Rosenfarb. After arriving in Montreal they had two children. Henry quickly earned a medical degree from the University of Montreal and by the mid-1950s had a family practice in the East End of Montreal. As he said years later, by the early '60s Henry had not only a good practice but a wife, children, and a mistress.

Morgentaler's early years experiencing anti-Semitism in Poland and then surviving war and the camps seemed to make him restless; he was searching for something. Maybe he would have had the same remarkable career had he not had those grim early experiences, but one suspects that those experiences somehow gave him the boldness and fortitude to defy the law and take extraordinary risks of his own freedom to help people in need. Perhaps it was because of the racial hatred and persecution he faced as a boy, even before the trauma of the ghetto and the camps. Polish kids would chase him and throw stones at him, and generally treated him as inferior. He once said, after he became a doctor, that he still felt an urge to prove that he was not a coward.

The early experiences seemed to have affected the two brothers in different ways. While Abraham wanted a safe life, Henry had an urge to find some way of making the world a better place.

Henry Morgentaler became bored and unhappy with his life as a doctor, successful though it was, and started searching for a cause to which he could commit himself. He found it in discovering the desperate need many women in Quebec had for abortions, which at the time were illegal in Canada. In 1967 he presented a brief, advocating a woman's right to a legal and safe abortion, to a House of Commons Health and Welfare Committee. Soon afterwards he started to get frequent calls from desperate women wanting abortions, which at that time could only be obtained with difficulty, in extreme circumstances. He had not realized the extent of the need. At first he declined the requests, citing the law. But he felt like a coward, and after hearing about the sometimes lethal results of botched amateur abortions, he felt he had to act. He would challenge the law.

In 1968 Morgentaler closed his family practice and, in defiance of the law, opened an abortion clinic. At first he was ignored by the authorities, some of whom may have realized the importance of the service provided by the clinic because of experiences of their own family members and friends. It is one thing to oppose abortion in theory; it is different when a person you are close to requires such help. So the clinic went on for two and a half years without disturbance, often getting referrals from other doctors.

On June 1, 1970, everything changed. The Montreal police raided the clinic. Certain Quebec officials had been badgering the police to do something. As the raid progressed and the police thoroughly searched the clinic, Morgentaler sat calmly eating a sandwich and drinking a Coke. He later said that his impulse in times of impending crisis, learned in the ghetto and the concentration camps, was to get something to eat to sustain him during the difficulties that lay ahead. The police charged Morgentaler with several counts of performing illegal abortions.

Morgentaler's lawyer was the renowned criminal lawyer Claude-Armand Sheppard. Sheppard's initial strategy was to stall — to use whatever delaying tactic he could think of — perhaps hoping that the law would be changed before his client was convicted. He knew his client was guilty of the charges against him; so did his client. So did everyone else. It was not a case Sheppard wanted to rush into. He was understandably nervous, thinking that regardless of public sympathy, his client would still face the inflexibility of the law, which he clearly had broken.

Morgentaler, however, grew impatient and wanted his day in court. But Sheppard kept forcing delays and three years passed. Like Morgentaler, Jerome Choquette, Quebec's Justice Minister, wanted action. But Choquette's reason was different from Morgentaler's: Choquette wanted Morgentaler to be punished for defying the law. Morgentaler, on the other hand, was seeking public vindication. He was confident, much more so than his lawyers, that the people would never find him guilty.

Finally, in frustration at the lack of legal action, Morgentaler decided to up the ante. Against Sheppard's advice, he gave a speech in Toronto on May 16, 1973, in which he announced that in the previous five years he had performed 5,000 abortions. The audience gasped. But still no legal action was forthcoming. Then he performed an abortion on television, essentially daring the police and prosecutors to do something about it. And all the while, throughout his three years of awaiting trial, he continued carrying on a full schedule of abortions in his clinic.

On August 15, 1973, the authorities moved in again, conducting a second and very well-organized raid on the clinic and arresting Morgentaler. He was released on bail, and he and Sheppard conferred to try to come up with some sort of credible defence. It was not immediately obvious what this would be. The prosecutors would not have to work very hard to prove their case: Morgentaler had already publicly admitted he had committed illegal acts. And he had performed one on public television! What could the defence do?

The charge against Morgentaler was based on what was at the time Section 251 (1) of the *Criminal Code of Canada*:

> *Everyone, who, with the intent to procure a miscarriage of a female person, whether or not she is pregnant, uses any means for the purpose of carrying out his intention is guilty of an indictable offence and is liable to imprisonment for life.*

This was a very serious threat. Morgentaler could have spent the rest of his years in prison. But, like William Penn centuries earlier (see Chapter 3), he was determined to risk everything to stand up to an unjust law. So Morgentaler and Sheppard went to court, with both of them, and everyone else involved, not having any idea of what was going to happen.

Well, maybe prosecutor Louis-Guy Robichaud thought he did. He appeared to be confident of a conviction. Just to be sure, however, he was careful in the jury selection process to eliminate all women of child-bearing age, thinking such women might be sympathetic to Morgentaler. Sheppard and his associate Charles Flam, on the other hand, had hoped to get a number of women on the jury, but managed only one.

Sheppard and Flam were more successful in finding jury members from Montreal's working class; these were people who, in Sheppard's words, "were in essentially difficult economic circumstances, people who faced real difficulties, were in daily conflict with the exigencies of life." They also wanted French-speaking jurors, even though they were likely to be Catholic, rather than English ones. They thought that working-class French jurors would better understand the problems associated with having no access to abortions. Sheppard and Flam also felt that, in spite of being predominately Catholic, French Canadians were more liberal in regard to social issues than English ones. Recent polls suggest this is still the case.

Morgentaler himself insisted that the trial be conducted in French, not for strategic reasons but because that was his normal language he used with his patients. This suited his lawyer's strategic ideas of selecting jury members. Perhaps suspecting what his opponents were up to, Robichaud objected, asking that the trial be held in English. He had little chance of winning that battle, however, at a time when feelings about the language to be used for public business in Quebec were running very high. Aside from the number of women chosen, Sheppard and Flam got the sort of jurors they wanted.

The trial began on October 18, 1973. Robichaud had initially received this assignment as part of a regular schedule — apparently he had not sought it out — but soon he appeared to become very emotionally involved. At times he was almost contemptuous, refusing at first to refer to Morgentaler as a doctor. He called him Mister Morgentaler. Perhaps adding to Robichaud's determination to get a conviction was pressure from Quebec Justice Minister Choquette, a hawk when it came to enforcing the law, and federal Justice Minister Otto Lang. Both ministers appeared anxious to see Morgentaler punished. Morgentaler had, after all, openly defied the law.

And he was openly provocative; some called him a gadfly.

The trial proceeded well for Morgentaler under the skilled guidance of Sheppard. Prosecutor Robichaud, on the other hand, seemed clumsy and inept. He bullied and treated his star witness with callous disregard for her difficult situation. She was Verona Parkinson, a poor, young, black student from Sierra Leone who had been dragged out of the clinic in the raid, shortly after her abortion.

Parkinson had few if any friends in Canada. She needed an abortion because she could not afford to raise a child and because she was afraid of the disgrace she would face if she had to go back home unmarried, with a child. She was a curious choice for the prosecution's star witness; she would have been a better choice as poster girl for the need for abortion on demand.

I was told by a lawyer who had been a young associate of Sheppard during the Morgentaler trials that Robichaud would have had a much better chance of winning jury support if the woman they had chosen to highlight their case had been well-off with no obvious financial need for an abortion. As it was, everyone could see that Parkinson was a woman in real need. Perhaps Robichaud was so sure of a conviction that he thought it did not matter.

Parkinson was bewildered by what was happening to her. She was liable for imprisonment herself simply for having had an abortion. After the raid she had been taken to a hospital for invasive examinations that should not have been made without her consent and which were not recommended for women with recent abortions. Morgentaler was so angry when he heard this that his lawyers could barely contain him.

Jury members, like most people in the courtroom, were, to say the least, unimpressed by Robichaud's insensitive treatment of this witness. Robichaud again showed bad judgment when he tried to paint Morgentaler as a foreigner, an outsider, who came to Canada and broke our laws. This strategy seemed gratuitous and offensive. Robichaud even tried, without success, to question Morgentaler's competence by bringing in a medical expert, a gynecologist, to testify against him. This was supposed to be key testimony for the prosecution, but the credibility of the gynecologist soon disintegrated when evidence was brought forward that he himself had referred eight patients to Morgentaler, including his own secretary. He had also answered a questionnaire from Morgentaler in which he had described the abortionist's skills as "excellent."

Robichaud's undistinguished performance continued when he brought in a motley array of anti-abortion fanatics, who mainly succeeded in making opponents of abortion seem rigid and unsympathetic, if not weird.

Robichaud insisted that the jurors must find Morgentaler guilty. "The law is the law," he said. One can imagine that the jurors, seeing the distasteful performance by Robichaud and his witnesses, and far from being turned off by Morgentaler's supposed arrogance and defiance, would be looking for a way, any way, to find him not guilty.

A key point in this trial was when Sheppard succeeded in convincing the judge to allow a defence based on Section 45 of the *Criminal Code of Canada*:

> **45.** *Every one is protected from criminal responsibility for performing a surgical operation on any person for the benefit of that person if*
>
> *(a) the operation is performed with reasonable care and skill; and*
>
> *(b) it is reasonable to perform the operation, having regard to the state of health of the person at the time the operation is performed and to all the circumstances of the case.*

This article had never been used in this way before; it was meant for situations such as emergency operations carried out at accident scenes and that sort of thing. But Sheppard made a convincing case for it and persuaded the judge to accept it. With that the jurors had all they needed to justify a verdict of not guilty, which is what they delivered. The date was November 13, 1973. Robichaud and his colleagues, and one can imagine Choquette and Lang as well, were incensed by what they saw as disregard for the law. They felt the Section 45 defence was not a legitimate one and was simply a pretext for a verdict of not guilty. They were probably right. The jurors did not want to convict Morgentaler, and they did not.

Because of the complicating factor of the judge accepting Section 45 as a defence, we cannot be sure that this first Morgentaler trial involved jury nullification. The jury almost surely did not want to convict Morgentaler and might not have done so even if the Section 45 defence had been disallowed — that would clearly have been nullification. But in this first trial, with the Section 45 argument accepted by the judge, the jury had a valid legal justification for their verdict. So we cannot argue that this verdict was based on nullification of the law.

On the other hand, it seems likely that the first jury would have refused to convict even if the Section 45 defence had not been allowed. Watching the shocking behaviour of Robichaud and his brutal treatment of the young woman from Sierra Leone, listening to his unreasonable anti-abortion witnesses, and then recognizing, with Sheppard's eloquent guidance, the heroic nature of Morgentaler's actions in helping women no one else would help, it is difficult to imagine a conviction. Morgentaler often said that a jury would never convict him.

While Morgentaler went right back to working in his clinic, Robichaud indicated his intention to appeal. This was to be expected, but the result of the appeal was extraordinary. Customarily a successful appeal of a jury decision leads to holding another trial, with a new jury. That would have been fair enough and, if wrong-headed, was at least within the bounds of reasonable legal procedures. But on this occasion the justices chosen to hear the appeal went much further than an appeal court had ever gone before. On April 26, 1974, the five justices handed down a unanimous judgment quashing the jury's verdict and replacing it with a guilty one. Morgentaler was immediately ordered to return to the trial court for sentencing.

There was a clause in the *Criminal Code of Canada* that permitted a judicial reversal of a jury decision, but it had never been used before. It is unlikely that any country with a legal system based on English law would have allowed such a thing; it undermined the whole purpose of a jury system. Jury decisions elsewhere, and previously in Canada, could be overturned so that another jury trial needed to be held, but never reversed. Never before had a panel of judges taken a jury verdict of not guilty and changed it to guilty.

The ruling of the Quebec Court of Appeals meant that the courts could simply nullify a jury when it did not like the jury's decision. This was an assault on the very idea of juries, on the long-standing notion, since Magna Carta and even earlier, of the right to a trial by a jury of peers. Nevertheless, Morgentaler was sent to prison. Many Canadians were justifiably outraged.

The five Appeal Court justices were all Roman Catholic and, some said, determined to punish Morgentaler for carrying out abortions. There were two Protestant judges on the Appeal Court, but they were excluded from this judgment. It all looked very much like an attempt to circumvent the jury system. Rather than jury nullifcation, this was nullification of a jury.

The assignment of a guilty verdict by the Appeal Court was a legal outrage, but the reasoning of the judges in regard to the not-guilty verdict did make some sense. They argued that the judge on the trial (Justice Hugessen) made an error in law by allowing a defence based on Section 45, which protects from criminal prosecution those who carry out surgical procedures. The justices correctly pointed out that Section 45 was meant for emergency situations, where an operation may be carried out in less-than-ideal conditions in order to save someone's life. They correctly related it to the defence of necessity, which has precedent in common law but is considered applicable only in extreme circumstances. Although Sheppard could make the case that getting an abortion in certain cases was a life-or-death matter, and therefore might be termed for legal purposes a necessity, it would be difficult to defend all cases of abortion in that way.

As much as Morgentaler's supporters, and Sheppard in particular, had welcomed Hugessen's ruling, it was not legally correct. The Appeal Court was essentially right in that respect, and had they simply ordered a new jury trial all would have been well. But maybe they sensed, correctly, that the jury, or any jury, would be reluctant to convict Morgentaler. Their intervention was almost surely taken to preclude nullification in a future trial.

Meanwhile, Morgentaler was given an 18-month sentence. He appealed to the Supreme Court of Canada, but the Court's role in such cases is not to decide if justice has been served but to determine if there have been any mistakes in law. There were none, at least none bad enough to overturn the Appeal Court's decision. The Appeal Court intervention and assignment of a verdict, while highly dubious, was legal. Morgentaler lost his Supreme Court appeal.

Morgentaler was stunned by the ruling; he had always felt that he would be protected by the people. But with the Quebec Court of Appeal's decision, and the Supreme Court upholding that decision, Morgentaler's fate was taken out of the hands of the people. He was now at the mercy of judges.

In March of 1975 he was sent to prison. It was a difficult time for Morgentaler, undoubtedly bringing back memories of Auschwitz and Dachau. At one point he, like William Penn so many years before him, was thrown into isolation. He suffered a mild heart attack during his isolation, an event that caused further outrage amongst his supporters.

Shortly after Morgentaler started serving his sentence, Quebec Justice Minister Choquette ordered a second trial. He had a list of abortion cases he could use to bring Morgentaler to trial; he could string these trials out for as long as he wanted. Perhaps by calling a new trial just after

Morgentaler went to prison he thought he might be able to mute some of the public criticism of the unprecedented judicial appeal process that had reversed the first jury's decision.

Moreover, since the Section 45 defence had been discounted by both the Quebec Appeals Court and the Supreme Court of Canada, it would be ruled inadmissible in any future trials. Choquette probably thought Morgentaler would be left with no plausible defence and that a new jury would convict him. If so, then the public outrage in regard to the Court of Appeals overturning the previous jury decision might have subsided. Thus not only would he be able to inflict further punishment on his antagonist Morgentaler, he might erase the black mark he carried as the person ultimately responsible for the questionable appeal decision. People might forget about that appeal if he could get a jury to convict in a second trial. Choquette needed a jury conviction.

He was not about to get it. He, like many others, probably misread the nature of the first jury's acquittal. Nullification was in the air.

Even Sheppard did not fully see this, perhaps wanting to think that his coming up with the Section 45 defence was the reason why the first jury did not convict. Having now lost that defence for the second trial and seeing no other obvious defence, he was very worried about what was going to happen next. While Morgentaler had his vociferous supporters, in the mid-1970s there were still many Canadians who were opposed to abortion. Banking on a jury that would unanimously agree to nullification must have seemed like a long shot.

With powerful politicians and judges lined up against his client, Sheppard was very concerned about the second trial. Even if he could get sympathetic jurors who would nullify the law, the Appeals Court could overturn a favourable jury decision anyway. Sheppard was so concerned that he advised his client to plead guilty. He was hoping to reduce the severity of the sentence Morgentaler would receive. Going on with the trial seemed to Sheppard to be too great a risk. It looked to him like the fight might be over and it was time to cut their losses.

Morgentaler, however, would have none of it. He knew he was not a criminal and he said he would never plead guilty.

As it turned out, all of them — Robichaud, Choquette, even Sheppard and his colleagues — underestimated the resolve of the juries they were dealing with. Sheppard of course had some sense of this — that is why he wanted a jury of working-class people who would understand the value of the service Morgentaler provided for these women. But he feared the power of the argument that the law is the law and he worried that jurors might give in to that power.

The second trial, with a different and more reasonable prosecutor, was less acrimonious, and in spite of his misgivings, Sheppard seemed to be winning the day. Left without his previous defence of Section 45, he concentrated on the argument of necessity, a defence that argues that Morgentaler had no alternative that to do what he did, for the sake of the women. This is a problematic defence because it is usually accepted only in extreme circumstances, like shooting someone who is about to shoot you. Still, Sheppard seemed to be getting away with it, with no objection from the trial judge, Justice Bisson.

However, Sheppard was shocked when Justice Bisson, in his final instructions to the jury, calmly said that it would be improper for jury members to consider any evidence that had been put forward for necessity, since such a defence was not available in this case. All they could do, he said, is decide if the defendant had violated Section 251 (which obviously he had), and that all other factors were irrelevant. Morgentaler later said that "until then Judge Bisson had seemed impartial and fair, and suddenly he almost ordered them to convict me."

Although Sheppard, his client, and his client's supporters were all stunned by the judge's instructions, they need not have worried. This second jury was not ready to convict any more than was the first. It was Morgentaler's second not guilty verdict in as many jury trials. This time the verdict came in the face of the main defence being called inapplicable by the presiding judge.

It was clear now that the juries in these trials, at least in the second and probably in the first, were nullifying the law against abortion. This second jury had no legal grounds to spare Morgentaler; he had done what was illegal and the judge had disallowed the main defence argument. But the jury members still refused to convict him.

That night family and friends celebrated the victory, but without Henry. He was back in prison, still serving his sentence given to him following the Appeal Court's decision in the first trial.

Morgentaler was winning the jury trials but losing wherever judges held the power. He was in prison despite two juries finding him innocent. He was eligible for parole in September 1975, after completing a third of his sentence, but the parole board turned him down, using other pending charges against him as the reason. These multiple pending charges were a means of controlling Morgentaler. Authorities, if they so wished, could have simply tried him on a single charge of multiple violations of Section 251 and, if he was found guilty, given him an appropriate sentence, which he could serve and then get on with his life. By reserving charges for a later date, however, they could go on charging him for a very long time and could keep him in prison as long as they wished. That is, they could if they could just get guilty verdicts.

Choquette was not about to give up. He ordered a third trial for Morgentaler, to great cries of alarm across the country. Was this not abuse of authority, with officials unfairly punishing a man whose juries refused to find him guilty? So far, with the two juries, the score was 24 to 0 in favour of Morgentaler. No matter. Choquette obviously disagreed with the juries and he had the power to continue harassing the doctor.

A main argument for jury independence is that an independent jury can act as a check on the abuse of power by authorities. It was argued this way in King John's time, in William Penn's time, and now in Henry Morgentaler's time. It is a powerful argument when we see such cases.

Still, though, there was the looming power of the Quebec Court of

Appeals to reverse the jury's verdict: the newly discovered power to nullify jury nullification.

Choquette's zeal in seeking prosecutions of Morgentaler, to say nothing of his hand in the scandal of the Appeal Court overturning the first verdict, were beginning to place him in bad repute across the country. The great orator John Diefenbaker, the former Progressive Conservative party leader, brought up the matter in Parliament. How, he demanded to know, could this man twice be found innocent but still be in jail? The Liberals were in power and Justice Minister Otto Lang, no friend of Morgentaler, was feeling the heat. He called the matter a "silly dispute" and promised a *Criminal Code* amendment to change the law so that a jury's verdict could not be overturned by a judicial appeal body; a new trial with another jury would then be the only route to reversing a jury's decision. But he buried the amendment in an omnibus bill that would take time for debate and passage, too much time to help get Morgentaler out of prison.

Morgentaler finally was released in February 1976, ten months after he was first sent to prison. Ron Basford had taken over from Otto Lang as federal Justice Minister in late 1975, and he had Morgentaler's questionable Appeal Court's conviction set aside, with the promise of a new trial to replace the one tainted by the judicial reversal of the jury verdict. Then Basford and the Trudeau government passed legislation in January 1975 prohibiting judicial reversals of jury verdicts. This became known as the Morgentaler Amendment to the *Criminal Code of Canada*.

The third trial for Morgentaler, in 1978, was the promised retrial of the first one, based on the original charges of the first trial. Again the new jury refused to convict a man who had clearly violated Section 251 of the *Criminal Code*.

Later in 1978, the Parti Québécois, which had taken power in Quebec two years earlier, declared Section 251 unenforceable. They dropped all charges against Morgentaler and announced that there would be no further prosecutions for abortions conducted by those with proper qualifications. Further, they asked the federal government to change the abortion law, although no such change was immediately forthcoming.

Reflecting on the trials, Sheppard made three points:

1) Juries play an important role in humanizing the law.

2) There comes a time when citizens will revolt against a bad law.

3) A determined individual can turn the system on its ear.

There was no doubt by this time that the Morgentaler juries were nullifying the law. They would not convict him no matter what defence was used or what the judges said about what was admissible as a defence. Morgentaler was not a criminal and juries would not convict him, whatever the law said. This was a great triumph for the idea of jury independence and jury nullification, the greatest in Canadian legal history. And many would argue that it was a great triumph for our legal system: even though of an unjust law, the system had found a way for justice to prevail.

In the 1980s Morgentaler took his campaign to other provinces, opening clinics first in Winnipeg and Toronto. Both were the object of protests and both were raided by the police, in spite of the Quebec government having declared the abortion law to be unenforceable. Protests in Winnipeg were led by Joe Borowski, an erstwhile politician and provincial cabinet minister in Schreyer's government in the late '60s and early '70s. In spite of his involvement with a left-leaning political party, Borowski was an adamant opponent of abortion and, among many other actions, took out a full-page newspaper ad condemning the new clinic. The clinic was raided and arrests were made, but prosecution was held off pending a similar action against the Ontario clinic.

Morgentaler's Ontario clinic opened on June 7, 1983, a few days after the Winnipeg clinic had opened. There was enormous publicity for the opening, provided mostly by the press who gave front-page coverage to the story. Morgentaler arrived at the opening to cheers from crowds of supporters. Protestors had decided not to attend, except for one who ran toward Morgentaler brandishing pruning shears. He was blocked by one of the abortion supporters and then ran off. Later he was arrested.

Incidents like the pruning shears highlighted the dangers to which Morgentaler constantly exposed himself, dangers that went beyond the possibility of imprisonment. In 2005 I was involved with organizing the annual meeting of the Humanist Association of Canada. Morgentaler had, years earlier, been given their Humanist of the Year award (the American Humanist Association similarly honoured him some years earlier) and he was invited to speak at the 2005 meeting. Even then, over 20 years after his last trial, special security precautions had to be taken.

At the meeting I was privileged to speak about that year's award winner, Evelyn Martens, about whom I had written extensively. Martens, like Morgentaler, was a courageous social activist who had been pros-ecuted in 2004 on two counts of assisting suicide. I was also asked to announce that Martens's award, and henceforth all future such awards, would be called "The Henrys." Morgentaler then handed out that year's "Henry" to Martens. I shall never forget sharing the stage with these two diminutive, aging people who had put themselves at so much risk in serving the desperate needs of those whom no one else would help. How much easier, I thought, to just write about these things; how much more difficult to actually put oneself out there on the front lines. It was a great but undeserved honour to stand up there with them.

Prior to the opening of the Toronto clinic, Morgentaler had been warned by his new lawyer in Toronto — the eminent, brilliant, and pro-gressive Morris Manning — that he would be breaking the law.

"Fine," Morgentaler is reported to have said. "Let's get on with it."

On July 5, 1983, just a few weeks after the clinic in Toronto opened, police staged a raid and removed a number of women, still shaky from having just undergone abortions, to waiting ambulances. The police then removed files and equipment. Morgentaler, who missed all of the excitement because he was on vacation in California, was charged with conspiracy to perform unlawful abortions. Two colleagues were similarly charged. The trial started on November 21, 1983.

Manning's strategy was to attack the abortion law under the recently passed Constitution of Canada with its *Charter of Rights and Freedoms*, a statement of legal principles that trumped all other laws in Canada. The *Charter* changed the role of judges in Canada from merely interpreting law to now determining the legitimacy of laws under the *Charter*. In pre-trial sessions Manning spent considerable time arguing that the judge in the trial, Judge William Parker of the Ontario Supreme Court, should take it upon himself to determine the unconstitutionality of the abortion law. Manning knew he might not succeed with this, but if not he would then have the advantage of having introduced the matter in the Ontario court, so it could subsequently be taken to the Supreme Court of Canada on appeal. He knew that a matter of this importance might well not be settled in lower courts. Judge Parker rejected the argument, although apparently it gave him cause to reflect upon the matter. It took him three months to decide. In the reasons for his judgment it was clear that he was almost persuaded by Manning, but appeared in the end unwilling to make the big decision about unconstitutionality. It appeared that he really agreed with Manning but thought such a major decision should go to higher courts.

On October 15, 1984, almost a year after the trial had first been sidetracked by the constitutional challenge, it began again. A full day was spent arguing over the rules that would be used to select jurors, because everyone knew that, as in the Quebec trials, the composition of the jury would be important in determining the outcome of the trial. There would be no disputing that Morgentaler and his colleagues had acted contrary to Section 251 of the *Criminal Code*; the question was would the jury find him guilty? So jury selection was a matter of more importance than usual.

The jury selection process was extraordinary. In Canada jury selection usually happens quickly with few if any questions allowed and few challenges. This one took three days, with Manning working with two jury selection experts from the United States. The American selection process is quite different from the Canadian, allowing many more questions of prospective jurors. Manning, knowing the critical importance of who was selected in this trial, wanted to persuade Judge Parker to give him much more leeway than normal in asking questions.

Manning gave Parker a list of fifty questions that he would like to ask each prospect. Parker rejected that idea, but it may have made him a bit more lenient in permitting some questions. Maybe that was Manning's strategy: to ask for the sky and end up with a bit more room. Manning argued that in a case of this importance, with so much emotional baggage, extra care needed to be taken to get an impartial jury. He would not, of course, have minded if the jury's impartiality was in his client's favour, but he knew that having any jury members implacably opposed to abortion would seriously hurt his client's cause.

Parker could see this and did take the unusual step of allowing questions about the candidates stand on abortion. One woman answered, "Well what do you think? I am a Catholic." Dodged a bullet on that one, Manning must have thought, as he rejected her. Not that any Catholic would have been rejected; Manning knew that Catholics are generally as open to abortion as other people. But this one was too determinedly Catholic.

Another candidate was wearing a lapel pin that caught Manning's eye. He asked what it was; it was a right-to-life insignia. Another bullet dodged. He was able to ask another woman if she used the title of Miss, Mrs., or Ms. "Mrs.," she said, a little too firmly.

Manning ended up with a jury he was comfortable with: six women and six men.

Prosecutor Allan Cooper based his case on two points, one legal and the other emotional. The first point was that Morgentaler and his colleagues were guilty of a conspiracy to commit a crime, something that could easily be proven by records that had been seized and by Morgentaler's own speeches. Secondly, Cooper argued that the clinics were essentially an expression of greed, not compassion — that Morgentaler made a lot of money from them. He was hoping to counter jury support for Morgentaler, but this claim that one sometimes hears from Morgentaler detractors had little credibility. There are a lot easier and safer ways for a doctor to make money.

Manning also made a straight legal argument and an emotional argument, but unlike Cooper's his emotional one had some justification. The legal argument was again the somewhat shaky one of necessity that Sheppard had used before him. But his case was shakier in one way because of the prosecution's clever tactic of charging Morgentaler and his colleagues with conspiracy to commit a crime rather than committing the crime itself. This meant that only evidence of the conspiracy could be brought forward, not evidence of performing abortions: no women were brought forward as proof. The conspiracy gambit deprived Manning of a Verona Parkinson, the young woman from Sierra Leone who, although a witness for the prosecution, served for the defence as an impressive example of the need for an abortion service.

Manning's emotional argument, then, became all-important. It had been a subtext in the Sheppard trials as well, but was more explicit here: Morgentaler was a good man committing acts of human kindness. He was not a selfish money-seeking criminal, but a good Samaritan. As Morgentaler said on the stand, he was driven by:

> The image of someone drowning on a river or lake, and all you had to do was to stretch out your arm to save them. Would you do it if there was a sign saying "it is forbidden to help"? I knew I could not obey that sign. I would obey a higher morality.

Then, in his closing address Manning got very specific about the jury's right to nullify the law, telling them clearly that whatever the law said, it was up to them and them alone to decide if they wanted to find Morgentaler and his colleagues guilty or not guilty.

In his instructions to the jury Judge Parker challenged the defence of necessity, but got particularly incensed in questioning Manning's suggestion that the jury could ignore the law. After the jurors left for deliberation Manning questioned Parker, saying, "your lordship's charge [instruction to the jury] completely and utterly takes away the defence."

Manning particularly objected to Parker's assertion that the jurors would be breaking the law if they returned a verdict of not guilty. This was wrong, he said, and it violated long-standing principles of British and Canadian law. Parker relented slightly and gave a new charge to the jury.

As with Sheppard before him, however, Manning need not have worried about what the judge told the jury. What Morgentaler had often said was apparently true: no jury would convict him.

After six hours the jury came back with a verdict of not guilty. Now it was Morgentaler 48, Prosecution 0.

A familiar pattern of jury acquittal and judicial appeal followed, with the Ontario Court of Appeal overturning the verdict, although this time because of the Morgentaler Amendment they could not reverse it. Instead they ordered a new trial. Before this could happen, however, the Supreme Court of Canada heard an appeal of the Ontario Appeal Court's decision, launched by Morgentaler and Manning. This was their big chance to change the abortion law in Canada.

The Court was split from the beginning. Manning knew some of the judges were angry about the defence he had used in the Morgentaler trial. One elderly and very conservative judge had, after the initial trial, taken the unusual and inappropriate step of going to Judge Parker and demanding that he charge Manning with contempt of court, both for his appeal for nullification and for his criticism of Parker's charge to the jury. Parker, to his credit, did not do so. He kept quiet about this unseemly intervention, which he thought would remain between the two men. Sometime afterwards Manning and Parker happened to be driving to a conference together. Manning mentioned to Parker that it was a good thing Parker had not pursued the contempt charge against him.

"How did you know about that?" the astonished Parker exclaimed.

"Well I do know," Manning said. "And it is a good thing for you that you did not do it, because I would have challenged it all the way to the Supreme Court, and I would have won."

The offending Supreme Court justice, who should have known better than to take a matter directly to a lower court justice, apparently made the further mistake of talking to one or more of his Supreme Court colleagues, and word leaked to Manning. If nothing else, this episode, which could have blown up into a legal scandal, served to demonstrate to Manning what he would be dealing with at the Supreme Court.

But Manning had been before the Supreme Court many times before and was very comfortable there. He wanted more time than the Court was prepared to allow, ending up with seven and a half hours, which turned out to be enough. He had fifteen points he wanted to make, giving him a half hour for each. He progressed through the first several points, on schedule, with hardly a question from the nine judges. These all had to do with abortion. Then he got into points touching on nullification, and the panel came alive. It was as though this, not abortion, had become the central issue. Strangely it seemed to animate the judges much more than any of the other topics at hand.

But abortion was the central issue, and by a vote of five to two they ruled that the Canadian law on abortion, Section 251 of the *Criminal Code*, was a violation of the *Charter of Rights and Freedoms*. The ruling decriminalized abortion in Canada (see Chapter Notes) and overturned the convictions of Morgentaler and his colleagues.

This important Supreme Court ruling came out on January 28, 1988.

* * *

Henry Morgentaler and Morris Manning are responsible for the decriminalization of abortion in Canada, and for improving the lives of many thousands of women and their families. Because of what the two of them accomplished, Morgentaler has been the recipient of many honours and awards, in addition to the ones mentioned above. In 2005, amid petitions both opposing and supporting him, he received an honourary doctorate from the University of Western Ontario. In 2008 he was awarded the Order of Canada, prompting three Catholic members of the Order to give up their memberships.

Morris Manning, appointed Queen's Counsel in 1978, has appeared before the Supreme Court of Canada over 100 times and before various superior courts and courts of appeal hundreds of times. He has been editor of several Canadian law reports, is the author of three legal texts, and co-authored the first Canadian text on criminal law. He has written many law articles and served on many legal panels, commissions, task forces, and committees. He has served as defence counsel in many high profile Canadian legal cases.

Morgentaler and Manning did more for Canada than making abortions available to Canadian women: they showed that juries can effectively fight against laws that are seen to be unjust. Many saw this as a great victory for our justice system; it showed, as Claude-Armand Sheppard said, that "juries play an important role in humanizing the law." Many celebrated this newly vindicated source of justice trumping rules and procedures. Many still celebrate this legal triumph by Morgentaler and Manning, this example of juries humanizing the law, as a shining moment in the administration of justice in Canada. But the Supreme Court of Canada did not hold it in such high regard. They squashed it.

CHAPTER 5

THE SUPREME COURT OF CANADA NULLIFIES NULLIFICATION

For who would bear . . . the insolence of office . . .

Hamlet

In 2009 when I was working on my book about Robert Latimer, who was convicted in 2000 for murder in Canada's most famous case of mercy killing, I visited Latimer in his apartment in Victoria. I had talked to Latimer several times in the mid-2000s when he was still incarcerated at William Head prison near Victoria, and then again on a number of occasions later in the decade when he was out on day parole in Victoria. Day parole allows people convicted of crimes to live a more normal life in a community, but with certain restrictions, including living in a designated halfway house. In Victoria the halfway house was in an unpleasant and noisy area of downtown frequented by an odd mixture of street people, drug dealers, and tourists. Latimer wisely rented an apartment on Gorge Road, a few kilometres away, where he would spend as much time as possible, returning to the halfway house only when required, which was most nights.

That day when I was talking to Latimer in his apartment I happened to mention something about the Morgentaler case. Latimer thought hard and then said he remembered his lawyer saying something about that case, but he could not remember exactly what it was. He did recall, however, that there was something good about the Supreme Court ruling (the 1988 ruling decriminalizing abortion) and something bad.

I was struck by the comment. I could remember the good part but what was the bad? What could be bad about that decision? Could Latimer or his lawyer have been opposed to abortion? Didn't seem likely, and if they had been, what would they have seen as the good part? The Court's decision was universally praised by supporters of abortion, and despised by opponents. For neither group, I thought, was there both good and bad in the ruling. There was either good or bad, not both.

I decided to look into it and read the judgment over again. The good part was easy to find. Because of Henry Morgentaler's actions, and those of two other doctors who worked with him in his clinics (Dr. Leslie Franck Smoling and Dr. Robert Scott), the Supreme Court ruled against the constitutionality of the Section 251 of the *Criminal Code of Canada*, the section which allowed abortions only under quite restrictive conditions. The challenge to Section 251, initiated by Morgentaler and his lawyer, Morris Manning, was based on the 1982 *Canadian Charter of Rights and Freedoms*, and in particular Clause 7 of that Charter:

> **7.** *Everyone has the right to life, liberty and security of the person and the right not to be deprived thereof except in accordance with the principles of fundamental justice.*

This ground for appeal had not been available to Morgentaler and his lawyers in his previous Supreme Court appeal following his first conviction in Quebec in 1975. The Court at that time stated that it was up to legislators to determine the law in regard to abortion. But in 1988, with the new *Charter* in hand, it was a different story. As Chief Justice G.B.

Dickson wrote in the judgment:

> *Canadian courts are now charged with the crucial obligation of ensuring that the legislative initiatives pursued by our Parliament and legislatures conform to the democratic values expressed in the Canadian Charter of Rights and Freedoms.*

Therefore the Court could now intervene in overturning laws, if those laws contravened the *Charter*. Consequently the court ruled that:

> *Forcing a woman by threat of criminal sanction to carry a fetus to term unless she meets certain criteria unrelated to her own priorities and aspirations is a profound interference with a woman's body and thus a violation of the security of the person.*

Section 251 and the previous convictions of Morgentaler and the other doctors were all struck down by this ruling, to great joy and celebration by many pro-choice activists across the country, to say nothing of many women in immediate need of an abortion. This was not just another legal victory; this was a victory that vastly improved the lives of a great many people. Those helped included women like Verona Parkinson from Sierra Leone who was dragged out of Morgentaler's Montreal clinic and given invasive and dangerous post-abortion examinations prior to testifying at Morgentaler's first trial. But those helped in the years following the historic Supreme Court decision included thousands of women of many different backgrounds, all faced with carrying, bearing, and raising of children they neither intended nor wanted to have. In many cases women were left to deal alone with this prospect of coping, for the rest of their lives, with the consequence of a brief sexual encounter. Even when there was a responsible man to share the burden, a new child could severely exacerbate the financial problems of the parents, often in families with already too many mouths to feed. And the ruling saved many desperate women from the grim and dangerous prospect of resorting to abortions carried out by unqualified practitioners.

But the Supreme Court decision was more than all of these things. It established the personal autonomy of women whose bodies were previously subject to controls devised and enforced by others (mostly men). Although there were and still are many who dissent, mostly on religious grounds, the decision was a very significant moment in the history of the emancipation of Canadian women.

Like most of my friends and acquaintances I have always thought very positively about that Supreme Court decision. It seemed to me a rare instance where the world, or a small part of it here in Canada, was distinctly improved by an official action. My friends and I all spoke in reverential tones when referring to Morgentaler, whose bravery led to the change; to Morris Manning, who engineered the victory; and to the Supreme Court justices, who actually brought it about. We felt good about Chief Justice Dickson and his compatriots on the court who supported the decision.

As I read through the first part of his ruling I loved the straightforward good sense of Dickson's comments, for example that the waiting time of one to six weeks for therapeutic abortions, allowed by Section 251, "may not seem unduly long, but in the case of abortion, the implications of any delay . . . are potentially devastating." Hurrah for Dickson and the Court. He — they — did a very good thing.

But as I continued to read I came across a section I had never noticed or heard about before, a section that, I thought, might not make Canada a better place. It is usually overlooked in the ruling, because of the much more sensational part decriminalizing abortion. It was signalled by the court's strangely animated discussion of the portion of Manning's presentation that touched on nullification, mentioned in the last chapter.

After his gratifying disposition on the right of women to have abortions, Dickson gives, starting on page 76, a lengthy commentary on defence lawyer Manning's address to the jury in the trial. Dickson writes,

"I find the argument [made by Manning] so troubling that I feel compelled to comment." He is referring to this statement by Manning:

> *The judge will tell you what the law is. He will tell you about the ingredients of the offence, what the Crown has to prove, what the defenses may be or may not be, and you must take the law from him. But I submit to you that it is up to you and you alone to apply the law to this evidence and you have a right to say it shouldn't be applied.*

This was the most explicit appeal for jury nullification in any of the four Morgentaler trials, although such an appeal was certainly the subtext in the three previous trials in Montreal. Sheppard in those trials used necessity as his main line of defence, but that was not viewed by any of the judges as a legitimate defence and was explicitly ruled out in the second trial. The judges, as they tell juries, are the arbiters of law, and therefore, legally speaking, there was no defence. Yet the juries acquitted Morgentaler in every case in Quebec, as they did in Ontario. Clearly this was jury nullification: the juries refused to accept the verdict that was directed by law.

Rather than explicitly argue for nullification, Sheppard provided a pretext — a disallowed defence — that made the juries more comfortable with a not guilty verdict. Manning on the other hand took no chances that his message would be misunderstood, or that his jury would, in ignorance, feel obliged to find a verdict of guilty. He stated the case for nullification clearly and unambiguously, and he stated the truth. This is what so troubled Dickson.

When I first read this section of the Morgentaler judgment I thought that Dickson must have good reasons for being so bothered about Manning's statement. He did not have to comment on the statement at all; it was not germane to the real issue at hand, which was the decriminalization of abortion. Dickson's comments on jury nullification are what is known as *obiter dictum*, a judicial aside that is not a necessary part of the main ruling.

Dickson must have had some really good reasons, I thought, for objecting so strongly to a truthful comment by Manning. We do not know what the jury's verdict would have been without Manning's statement about nullification, but that statement may well have been the trigger for acquittal that led to the Supreme Court's ruling and the legalization of abortion.

Moreover, as I read on I realized that Dickson was not only troubled by Manning's statement; he was, in effect, issuing a ban on all future such statements by defence lawyers. As I realized the significance of Dickson's statement, I imagined he surely must have had really, really good reasons for taking such a strong position — a position which eliminated the possibility of a defence argument such as the one that had been central to the Morgentaler victory.

I read over Dickson's reasoning very carefully and will reproduce all of his relevant comments here, along with some brief reactions of my own. Later, in Chapters 7 and 8, I will analyze in more detail all of the arguments for and against jury independence and nullification.

Dickson: *The burden of his* [Manning's] *argument was that the jury should not apply s. 251 if they thought that it was a bad law, and that, in refusing to apply the law, they could send a signal to Parliament that the law should be changed.*

Comment: If there is a bad law that would lead to an unjust prosecution, then yes, many would say it should be opposed by a verdict of not guilty. One might also hope it would send a message to Parliament. That might have happened earlier in the Morgentaler case, when the three Quebec juries refused to convict. Appeals were made then to the federal government to change Section 251, including one from the Parti Québécois, but nothing happened. Parliament still has not changed the law banning abortions, although of course, given Dickson's ruling on abortion, Section 251 was struck down and is no longer enforceable.

Sending a message to government about how the law may not be aligned with community standards of justice is not a bad idea. However, I think, it is not generally a major motivation for juries to nullify the law. Mostly it is to avoid what appears to them to be an injustice.

Dickson: *It has long been settled in Anglo-Canadian criminal law that in a trial before judge and jury, the judge's role is to state the law and the jury's role is to apply that law to the facts of the case . . . It is a general principle of British law that on a trial by jury it is for the judge to direct the jury on the law and in so far as he thinks necessary on the facts, but the jury, whilst they must take the law from the judge, are the sole judges on the facts.*

Comment: This is the first of Dickson's real arguments, and it reflects a position that is repeated over and over again in the directions trial judges give to juries. Judges want juries to simply assess the facts in a case, determine then if the facts indicate a law was broken, and if so find a verdict of guilty. The idea is that judges are the experts in the law and therefore are the ones who should interpret the law for juries, which consist of lay people generally untrained in the law. Juries, the argument goes, should stick to what they can do as lay people, which is to assess the facts in a case. This is a tidy concept that is often used to discredit the idea of jury independence. It is, however, somewhat contradicted by Dickson's own next remark.

Dickson: *The jury is one of the great protectors of the citizen because it is composed of twelve persons who collectively express the common sense of the community. But the jury members are not expert in the law, and for that reason they must be guided by the judge on questions of law.*

Comment: Jurors are not experts in the law and ought to be guided by the judge on understanding what the law in a particular case says and means. It is crucial that the jury understand the law. Nullification, however, does not occur when jurors do not understand the law; it occurs when they understand the law but disagree with it. That is how, presumably, a jury can be "one of the great protectors of the citizen" by expressing the "common sense of the community." Dickson here seems to acknowledge the value of the independent perspective of a jury.

Dickson: *The contrary principle contended for by Mr. Manning, that a jury may be encouraged to ignore a law it does not like, could lead to gross inequities. One accused could be convicted by a jury who supported the existing law, while another person indicted for the same offence could be acquitted by a jury who, with reformist zeal, wished to express disapproval of the same law. Moreover, a jury could decide that although the law pointed to a conviction, the jury would simply refuse to apply the law to an accused for whom it had sympathy. Alternatively, a jury who feels antipathy towards an accused might convict despite a law which points to acquittal. To give a harsh but I think telling example, a jury fuelled by the passions of racism could be told that they need not apply the law against murder to a white man who had killed a black man. Such a possibility need only be stated to reveal the potentially frightening implications of Mr. Manning's assertions.*

Comment: There are some serious issues raised here that will be analyzed in Chapter 8, which looks at the various arguments made against jury nullification, including those by Dickson. Included then will be a discussion about different verdicts for the same offence and a detailed analysis of the troubling problem of racism and jury nullification (see Emmett Till, Chapter 2), which is still a possibility in a world where racism stubbornly persists.

Dickson then quotes from an often-quoted judgment by Lord Mansfield in a 1784 criminal libel case: *So the jury who usurp the judicature of law, though they happen to be right, are themselves wrong, because they are right by chance only, and have not taken the constitutional way of deciding the question. It is the duty of the Judge, in all cases of general justice, to tell the jury how to do right, though they have it in their power to do wrong, which is a matter entirely between God and their own consciences.*

Comment: Lord Mansfield is saying that it is always wrong for the jury to not follow the law, and if they happen to get something right by not doing so it is by accident only. The quote suggests that, without the letter of the law and the judge to guide them every step of the way, juries will get things right only by chance. The judge needs to tell them what is right, and if they do not follow the judge's guidance then they will have to answer to God for their wrongdoing.

While opponents of nullification are fond of this quote, it both convoluted and problematic. If jury members are simply to do what judges tell them to do, why, we might ask, should we have juries at all? If strict adherence to law overrides all other concerns, why not just have a panel of lawyers or judges make all the decisions? And if juries do not follow the judge's instructions, do they really need to ask for holy forgiveness in doing so?

Do the members of Morgentaler's four juries need to answer to God for what they did? Were the forty-eight people on those juries right "only by chance?"

Dickson quotes again from the same 1784 case: *To be free is to live under a government by law . . . Miserable is the condition of individuals, dangerous is the condition of the State, if there is no certain law, or, which is the same thing, no certain administration of law, to protect individuals, or to guard the State.*

Comment: Freedom does depend on rule by law, not by individuals. But this raises two questions:

1) Is it right that an exception should be made for juries? This entails an analysis of the main arguments for and against independence.

2) How would our justice system work if juries were not independent? Is it reasonable to have constraints put upon jury decisions?

Both of these questions will be addressed in detail in Chapters 7 and 8. Dickson again quotes from the 1784 case, with the additional comment "I can only add my support to that eloquent statement of principle":

In opposition to this, what is contended for? — That the law shall be, in every particular cause, what any twelve men, who shall hap-

pen to be the jury, shall be inclined to think; liable to no review, and subject to no control, under all the prejudices of the popular cry of the day, and under all the bias of interest in this town, where thousands, more or less, are concerned in the publication of newspapers, paragraphs, and pamphlets. Under such an administration of law, no man could tell, no counsel could advise, whether a paper was or was not punishable.

Comment: The suggestion here is that we would descend into anarchy if juries are allowed to be independent, and that popular and erratic opinion would carry the day. Although expressed in alarmist terms ("no man could tell"), the central argument against nullification is a legitimate one: the need for the rule of law. This concern is examined in detail in Chapters 8.

Dickson: *It is no doubt true that juries have a de facto power to disregard the law as stated to the jury by the judge. We cannot enter the jury room. The jury is never called upon to explain the reasons which lie behind a verdict. It may even be true that in some limited circumstances the private decision of a jury to refuse to apply the law will constitute, in the words of a Law Reform Commission of Canada working paper, "the citizen's ultimate protection against oppressive laws and the oppressive enforcement of the law" (Law Reform Commission of Canada, Working Paper 27, The Jury in Criminal Trials (1980)).*

Comment: Here Dickson acknowledges that, yes, juries ought to have the power to nullify the law and that nothing can be done about that. He is probably thinking about the absurdity of punishing juries, as at the William Penn trial. Most judges would probably, if pushed, agree with statement of the Law Reform Commission, that juries are *"the citizen's ultimate protection against oppressive laws."*

Dickson: *But recognizing this reality is a far cry from suggesting that counsel may encourage a jury to ignore a law they do not support or to tell a jury that it has a right to do so. The difference between accepting the reality of de facto discretion in applying the law and elevating such discretion to the level of a right was stated clearly by the United States Court of Appeals, District of Columbia Circuit, in United States v. Dougherty, 473 F.2d 1113 (1972), per Leventhal J., at p. 1134.*

Comment: Here is Dickson's argument that a defence lawyer should not be able to tell a jury that it can nullify the law, as Manning did in the last Morgentaler trial. Dickson makes much of a distinction between a jury having the "discretion" to nullify and having the "right" to do so. This distinction is key to Dickson's argument because if the ability to nullify is a right then surely juries should be informed about it — how can one justify withholding information about a right? If on the other hand nullification is a matter of "de facto discretion," then an argument to inform would be less compelling.

This goes to the heart of Dickson's main point — that defence counsel ought not to tell juries that they can nullify — and is dealt with at some length in Chapter 8 in the discussion of "Not a Right, Just a Power."

Dickson (quoting this time from the Dougherty appeal ruling): *The jury system has worked out reasonably well overall, providing 'play in the joints' that imparts flexibility and avoid[s] undue rigidity. An equilibrium has evolved — an often marvellous balance — with the jury acting as a 'safety valve' for exceptional cases, without being a wildcat or runaway institution. There is reason to believe that the simultaneous achievement of modest jury equity and avoidance of intolerable caprice depends on formal instructions that do not expressly delineate a jury charter to carve out its own rules of law.*

Comment: The argument here is that we have achieved a balance between juries acting as a final check on the law and juries going rogue and ignoring the law altogether. So juries do not need to be told they can disregard the law; it will happen if it should happen. However, read about the Robert Latimer case (see next chapter), and a further consideration of this point in Chapter 8.

Dickson*: To accept Mr. Manning's argument that defense counsel should be able to encourage juries to ignore the law would be to disturb the* *"marvellous balance"* of our system of criminal trials before a judge and jury. Such a disturbance would be irresponsible. I agree with the trial judge and with the Court of Appeal that Mr. Manning was quite simply wrong to say to the jury that if they did not like the law they need not enforce it. He should not have done so.

Comment: These are Dickson's final words on the matter. Is his argument a good one? Is it good enough to justify preventing defence lawyers from mentioning the nullification option to jurors? You decide, but again urge you to wait until you have read the rest of this book.

* * *

Dickson's opinion on nullification has had a chilling effect on the Canadian legal system. Lawyers like Mark Brayford in the Latimer case have felt constrained and unable to use a defence like the one used by Morris Manning in Morgentaler's last trial. Does this provide the best opportunity, or any opportunity, for juries to play the role for which they were created: to stand up against, in the words of the Law Reform Commission quoted by Dickson, "oppressive enforcement of the law"? Do the arguments Dickson provides justify limiting juries in the way that he has prescribed?

In Chapters 7 and 8 I will come back to a detailed analysis of the arguments for and against jury independence and to what extent juries should be informed of their rights in this regard. Then in Chapter 9 I will address Dickson's argument that nullification must not be mentioned in court and discuss what we as ordinary citizens might do about it.

Dickson's ruling on nullification is the "bad thing" about the Morgentaler ruling that Robert Latimer was trying to remember in our discussion a few years ago. It certainly was a bad thing for Latimer. Largely because of the Dickson ruling he was deprived of his best defence, given a life sentence, and sent to prison. Dickson's ruling is why Latimer was not living with his family and working his farm in Northern Saskatchewan, and was instead talking to me that day in his lonely apartment on Gorge Road in Victoria.

CHAPTER 6

LATIMER: GUILTY

Composite News story, November, 1999:

After nearly seven years of legal proceedings, including two trials and many appeals, Robert Latimer was found guilty of second degree murder and given a life sentence, with ten years before he is eligible for parole. When the jury foreman read the verdict Latimer's wife Laura cried out "no, no, no, no." In 1993 Latimer had ended the life of his severely ill daughter Tracy, in what many have called a mercy killing.

Overheard in the Latimer jury room:

"We can't just send him to prison — he is not a criminal. He is not a murderer," one juror said.

"Yes we can. We must. According to the law he is a criminal. He is a murderer," another juror said.

"But how can we?" the first juror asked.

"We have no choice," the second said.

This was not, of course, actually overheard. We cannot know exactly what was said in that jury room, because jurors in Canada are legally prevented from revealing what took place during their deliberations. But we can imagine something of what must have taken place in the courthouse in the small town of Battleford, Saskatchewan, in October and November of 1997.

The charge was second-degree murder, and at least some of the jurors were very uncomfortable with that. Maybe all of them were. This man, Latimer, was clearly not a murderer in the usual sense of the word. Murder suggests ending a life with malice, and that certainly did not apply in this case. Latimer ended the troubled life of his severely compromised daughter, Tracy, in order to relieve her of a painful and deteriorating existence that, Latimer believed, had no hope of improvement. This was a life in which the uncomprehending Tracy had already endured over twelve years of pain and discomfort, including the frequent dislocation of her hip joint by uncontrolled and sometimes violent muscle spasms.

But murder was the technically correct charge. In fact, according to the *Criminal Code of Canada*, first-degree murder would have been technically correct, and that actually was the charge in the first of Latimer's two trials. Latimer not only deliberately killed Tracy but did so after planning it for two weeks, ample time to be considered premeditation, the requirement for a first-degree conviction. First-degree murder carries a life sentence with a minimum of twenty-five years in prison before the possibility of full parole; second-degree murder has a minimum of ten years.

Latimer began serious planning for ending Tracy's life following a visit his wife, Laura, had made with Tracy on October 12, 1993, to the orthopedic surgeon Dr. Anne Dzus, who had been seeing Tracy since 1985. The Latimers and Dr. Dzus all knew that Tracy was going to require more surgery, even though her frail little body had already, in its twelve pain-wracked years, undergone several surgeries, including a major one a year earlier to relieve the severe scoliosis (curvature of the spine) Tracy had developed by the age of eleven. That operation, described as major surgery by Dr. Dzus, lasted seven hours as Tracy had steel rods inserted in her back to straighten her spine, which by this time had curved to 73 degrees out of alignment. Her internal organs were being crushed, threatening her survival. The rods got her spine back to within 15 degrees of alignment, allowing her to eat and breathe more freely, but they made her body rigid.

At the trial Laura had testified that after the surgery Tracy "was rigid as a board. Before the surgery she was flexible. You could sit and rock with her, and she loved to be rocked . . . Bob used to rock her for hours . . ."

It was fall harvest time when Laura took her daughter to the October 1993 appointment with Dr. Dzus; Robert did not go as he was busy in the fields, taking in the crops. They all knew that Tracy was going to need corrective work on her hip, which had been problematic for years. It seemed to be getting worse and was clearly causing the little girl a lot of pain. The right hip appeared to give Tracy the most trouble, although the left was damaged too. Dr. Dzus would have taken action on the hip earlier, but she was concerned that Tracy's frail body would not be able to tolerate another surgical intervention too soon after the trauma of putting the steel rods in her back.

A year had passed since the back operation, enough time that Dzus felt that action on Tracy's hip could be considered. Dzus was immediately struck by the pain Tracy was in. In her testimony at trial she said that when she came into the examination room Tracy "was lying on the examination table . . . her mother was holding her right leg in a fixed flexed position with her knee in the air and any time you tried to move that leg Tracy expressed pain, and her way of expressing pain was to cry out." Tracy could not speak about her pain because she had the mental capacity of a four- or five-month-old baby.

Robert and Laura thought that the treatment was going to be reconstructive surgery — reassembling the ball and socket in the hip joint. But X-rays showed the hip was too far-gone for that: the joint was too badly eroded and the cartilage too worn. One wonders how much pain this deteriorating condition, this erosion of bone and stretching and tearing of tissues, had brought to Tracy over the years.

The only recourse at this point, Dzus said, was a "salvage job": removing part of the socket and cutting off the top quarter of her femur to eliminate all bone-to-bone contact. This would leave what is known as a "flail joint," which would not support her weight, but then she never could walk anyway. The operation is known as resection arthroplasty. Feeling that the need for this operation was urgent, Dzus found a cancellation in her schedule so that the operation could be carried out as soon as possible — in two weeks.

The operation, however, was not going to end the pain. Dzus explained that "the post-operative pain can be incredible. In the hospital it could be mitigated by using epidural catheters to freeze the lower half of the body." This treatment could not go on too long, however, and the child would have to go home and just suffer the pain. As was the case throughout her life, it was not possible for Tracy to take strong pain medication, because of other medication she had to take to minimize the convulsions that had plagued her from birth, or at least from the time she was resuscitated after her birth. It was believed that stronger pain relievers would conflict with what she was already taking and could be fatal. So Tracy was allowed no pain reliever stronger than Tylenol 2.

Recovery from the operation, Dzus said, would take "a good year, and maybe even longer." But by then the other hip would probably need to be done, as well as other likely treatments such as inserting a feeding tube into Tracy's stomach to help cope with her faulty swallowing mechanism.

Laura was not prepared for this. To an outsider the prospect of one or maybe two more operations might not seem so bad, but to Laura the news of this unexpectedly invasive procedure, this cutting off of her daughter's leg bone, was devastating. Maybe the seemingly endless frustration and heartbreak finally got to be too much. After years of deterioration, Tracy would now undergo this "mutilation," as Laura saw it, with more to come in the future. Laura was stunned by the news. She was in despair. She could not stop crying.

Laura managed to return home and get dinner for Robert and her three other children (all younger than Tracy), but she said nothing about the doctor until she and Robert had gone to bed. Then she told him. He was distraught. For over twelve years it had been bad news piled upon bad news. It was like an ever-worsening nightmare, except it was one that they never woke up from. They were plagued by a feeling of helplessness.

On November 23, 1980, the lifeless body of Tracy Latimer was extracted from her mother using forceps, because at some point during her birth her heart had stopped beating and the blood supply to her brain had been cut off. A faulty heart monitor had caused confusion between the baby's heartbeat and the mother's. The staff at the small hospital in North Battleford did not notice the problem at first, but when they did they hurriedly extracted the baby's body. It was too late: considerable brain damage had already occurred. Laura said the baby was "flat, just literally flat . . . and they started to work on her right away, they got her breathing . . . I wasn't to hold her or anything, but they did allow me to see her for a minute, and then they took her away."

Such traumas to the brain of a baby result in the condition known as cerebral palsy. Most cases are relatively mild and allow those who have it to lead normal lives. But some cases, like Tracy's, are very severe and allow nothing resembling a normal life. At first no one knew how bad it was for Tracy, but early on Robert noticed her fingers twitching. This was a sign of the seizures Tracy would suffer throughout her life. There was a constant struggle to find medications that would control the convulsions but not cause too much collateral damage to the tiny body of the child.

Dr. Dzus described Tracy's condition as "one of the worst forms of cerebral palsy in that she was totally body-involved. Her total body was involved from her head right down to her toes, so all four limbs, her brain, her back, everything was involved." This meant that most of her movements were spastic and uncontrolled. While milder cases — most cases of cerebral palsy — do not usually result in cognitive problems, severe ones sometimes do, and Tracy's brain would never develop beyond that of a young baby.

Although this was an almost unmitigated tragedy, Robert and Laura loved their compromised daughter and would have done anything for her. Tracy actually brought Robert and Laura closer together. As Laura said, "if one got depressed the other person would be up and say we'll get through this . . . Tracy will get through, we'll be all right." Still, Laura cried herself to sleep every night for a year, grieving over what had happened to her baby.

Life was difficult: Tracy could never do anything for herself. She could recognize her parents and her siblings and would sometimes respond positively by smiling when she saw them, when she was not in too much pain. But the little girl was not getting better and she would never do so; it was a struggle just to keep her alive and as comfortable as possible as she continued to deteriorate.

After the crushing news from Dr. Dzus at the meeting on October 12, 1983, both Robert and Laura were in despair. It seemed like they had come to a point where they could do nothing more to protect their daughter from these new surgical invasions of her body and from the worsening descent into uncontrolled pain.

Well, there was one thing they could do, and it passed through Laura's head that night, after the meeting with Dr. Dzus. She said to her husband, "Maybe it is time to call Dr. Kevorkian." She said no more about it, but the idea was planted in Robert's mind. There was no other solution for Tracy, nothing else that would really help her. And he knew he had to do it alone; he did not want Laura or anyone else to be implicated should legal trouble arise. He knew that Tracy's poor, sad, troubled, uncomprehending life was no longer a life worth living. He was convinced that the best thing he could do for her was to end her life. That night he started thinking about how he would do it.

Robert Latimer faced a dilemma more wrenching than anything most of us will ever face. His critics, and there are many of them, have never lived in his shoes. It is easy to say that he should have simply let his daughter go on living as long as she could, but all that meant was to prolong her suffering. Robert knew by this time that there was really no hope for a decent life for Tracy — just more pain and, as he and Laura saw it, mutilation. There was not the slightest doubt in his mind that the best thing, *for Tracy,* was to end her life.

Laura undoubtedly felt much the same way, although it is doubtful that she could have ended her daughter's life herself. Apparently she knew nothing of Robert's plan and was angry when she found out what he had done, not because she wanted Tracy to live on, but because she realized the likely serious legal consequences. She was actually happy when she found Tracy's dead body in her little bed where Robert had placed her after she died.

"Finally Tracy had a break," she said.

In her testimony Laura also said:

> I wished it [death] for her every day. I can remember lying in the tub, and I'm thinking I wished I had a shot [an injection] or something for her, but I knew I didn't have the courage to do it, but I wished it for her. I wished it for her every day. I was her mom and that's what I wanted for her.

This was a mother who, like most mothers, wanted the best for her child. Sadly, she knew that, in Tracy's case, the best thing was death. Robert knew it as well, and he knew that Laura knew it too.

I think about Tracy sometimes, not because I want to but because the image of this uncomprehending child trapped in a dysfunctional body, suffering untreatable pain, is a haunting one. And at the same time another image slips into my mind: some years ago I happened to hear a Catholic priest speaking to some gathering about euthanasia. "Pain and suffering," he said, "are not necessarily such bad things." I have difficulty imagining anything good about the suffering of a helpless child like Tracy.

After the rest of his family had gone off to church on Sunday, October 24, 1983, just under two weeks after the fateful meeting with Dr. Dzus and one day before Tracy's scheduled hip operation, Robert took Tracy from her bed and into the cab of his truck. He turned the engine on and used a hose to direct the exhaust into the cab. He climbed into the back of the truck to watch what was happening, intending to pull Tracy out if she seemed in any distress. He had heard that carbon monoxide poisoning was not a stressful way to die, but he wanted to be sure Tracy did not suffer. She died very peacefully and Robert then removed her to her bed so no one else, including Laura, would know what he had done; it would look like Tracy had just died in her sleep.

Robert, however, was not a good criminal. Deception was not in his character. The police immediately suspected what had happened, guessing that she had been poisoned by carbon monoxide because of the telltale pinkness of Tracy's flesh. Later tests of Tracy's blood showed a high level of carbon monoxide. After denials during the initial interrogation Robert quickly conceded and soon was escorting the police around the property showing them exactly what he had done. Despite repeated urging by the police he refused to consult a lawyer, until after he had told the police everything.

At intervals the police would ask, "Do you wish to call a lawyer now?"

"Not really, no," Latimer would say.

When he finally did bring in a lawyer, it was a real estate lawyer he knew. Later he engaged criminal lawyer Mark Brayford, who was distressed by how much his client had given away and tried to get that material excluded from the evidence at trial, but was unable to do so.

Latimer does not see himself as a criminal. He just does not see himself that way and did not throughout the police investigation and the subsequent trials and appeals. He believes what he did was done out of necessity; there was no other way to help his daughter out of the situation she was in. Getting a defence lawyer, the first thing that would occur to most of us, just did not seem necessary to Latimer.

And he is not a criminal in any sense except a technical one. He is a good man who did what he thought he had to do, for the sake of his daughter.

The legal consequences, however, turned out to be severe. The case against Latimer was not hard to prove: he "murdered" his daughter in violation of Section 229 of the *Criminal Code of Canada* and he had done so in a premeditated manner. There was no doubt about any of this; those facts were not contested. Conceivably there might have been some sort of defence based on interpretation of what had happened, if Latimer had not already admitted everything, but it is unlikely Latimer would have allowed that anyway. He was an honest man and would have had great difficulty trying to slip out of the charges using some tricky legal manoeuvre.

Brayford's defence was that Latimer had to do what he had to do: it was a necessity. What else could he plead? But such a defence was never going to carry the day, any more than it carried the day for Morgentaler. Morgentaler was found not guilty because his juries knew he was not a criminal, and they believed that he broke the law for reasons of compassion. The necessity defence was a pretext; the real reason for acquittal was his jury's simple refusal to call the man a criminal. As Morris Manning had argued in the last Morgentaler trial, "*it is up to you and you alone to apply the law to this evidence and you have a right to say it shouldn't be applied.*"

This was Latimer's only real hope for acquittal: that the jury would say that in this case the law should not be applied — in other words, jury nullification. Except that now, after Chief Justice Dickson's proclamation about jury nullification in the Supreme Court's 1988 Morgentaler judgment, defence lawyers felt they could no longer mention the possibility. As defence lawyer Eddie Greenspan said in Latimer's final Supreme Court appeal, juries can practice nullification, you just can't tell them about it.

The jury could see that this was a tragic circumstance — tragic for Tracy living in her terribly compromised body, tragic for the Latimers watching their daughter suffer, increasingly so, as the years dragged on. But the *Criminal Code* left no room for compassion for these people, or for sympathetic interpretation of the law: Latimer was guilty of murder.

Latimer actually had two full trials. I will focus mostly on the second, which is the one that counted, but there are a few points of interest in the first. There was some indication that the jury in Latimer's first trial was to some degree sympathetic, even though the prosecutor in that trial, Randy Kirkham, was very hostile to Latimer. During the trial he referred to Latimer in an extraordinary way, describing him as "foul, callous, cold, calculating, and not motivated by anything other than making his own life easier."

Kirkham was later criticized by the Saskatchewan Court of Appeal for making such intemperate and unsupported comments. In his prosecutorial zeal Kirkham agreed to having Latimer charged with first-degree murder, refusing to use his discretion for a lesser charge as has previously happened in mercy-killing cases or, for example, when battered woman have killed their abusers. The appropriate charge in such cases has often been determined, by fair-minded prosecutors, to be manslaughter. This does not allow the taking of a life to go unpunished, but it allows for much more leniency in sentencing. Even second-degree murder has a minimum sentence of ten years in prison before eligibility for full parole.

Had Latimer been charged and convicted of manslaughter he probably would have been given a token one-year sentence, or something like that, served his short sentence and then have gone on with the rest of his life. The whole affair would be more or less forgotten by now. But a life sentence for murder is a different matter; it requires at least ten years of incarceration and a lifetime on parole. It can be a life-killer.

We do not know if the jury in the first trial considered a verdict of not guilty, or if they knew they could, but they did show some sympathy for

Latimer in rejecting Kirkham's plea for first-degree murder. In spite of first-degree being the legally correct charge, they found Latimer guilty of second-degree murder, which some have seen as a mild version of jury nullification. Going by the letter of the law would have led them to a conviction for first-degree murder.

There were more prosecutorial hijinks in the first trial. When the case was under appeal with the Supreme Court of Canada, it came to light that Kirkham and the police had engaged in the illegal business of pre-screening potential jurors, sending out questionnaires to potential jury members asking them about such things as their religious beliefs. Such questions, even in the official process of jury screening, are not allowed in Canada. On hearing of this during the appeal (both Latimer trials went to appeal, first to the Saskatchewan Court of Appeals and then to the Supreme Court of Canada) the Supreme Court ordered a new trial — hence the second trial.

Kirkham's harsh words and his pre-screening of jurors were mistakes not repeated by the second prosecutor, Eric Neufeld. The jurors at the second trial heard no such scathing indictments of Latimer, at least not at the trial; Neufeld was much more circumspect in his comments. But before the trial the jurors likely had heard some of the negative commentary about Latimer. They may have read about Kirkham's comment above or another comment he had made in the trial:

[murdering Tracy] *should be no different here in this case than it would be if* [Latimer] *had murdered* [their new] *baby Lee, who was two to three months old at the time Tracy's life was taken. Why should it be any different? We would not tolerate this conduct or have, I suggest, a moment's hesitation were it baby Lee, Lindsay or Brian Latimer as the victim. Your decision in this case should be no different just because Tracy had cerebral palsy. It is not open season on the disabled.*

Disability of course was not the issue. Tracy had been severely disabled for almost thirteen years, and both parents had continued to give her loving care for all of that time.

Some people still feel that severe punishment was due just so that people would not think it was "open season on the disabled," as Kirkham said. Some people have hardened their hearts against Latimer by thinking, as some critics claimed, that what he did was done just to save himself and his family from the onerous task of caring for Tracy. Many people have previously heard or read the views of some media commentators who strongly condemned Latimer for what he did, and made all sorts of ill-informed negative allegations about his motives.

To have a balanced and accurate perspective on the Latimer case it is necessary to know what kind of man he is. The charges by his critics are all possible for some defendants, but not Latimer. We know this because of the loving care that he had given Tracy for over twelve years, and because of the evident distress he felt at the deteriorating and grim and painful situation Tracy was in and was facing in the future. And we know what kind of man he is from people who, unlike Kirkham, actually knew him.

When Dr. Dzus was asked at trial to describe the manner in which her parents had cared for Tracy though her lifetime, she said:

> *I had no concerns about the way Tracy was being cared for. I think she came from a very caring, loving environment that looked out for Tracy.*

When Brayford asked her if she ever perceived that they had anything but her best interests at heart, she simply said no.

There was lots of other evidence to this effect, and nothing that suggested otherwise. Latimer himself wrote:

> *Cruelty to Tracy was no longer something we could tolerate . . . The brutal description of cutting a large portion of Tracy's leg off was unthinkable to us . . .*

We spent years trying different drugs independently, in combinations, and in various dosages. We had to drive to Saskatoon very often, sometimes just for her blood to be tested to gauge the level of the drug in her system, and back the next day to see a doctor to adjust the dosage, or change to a different drug. We probably averaged two to four trips to the hospital in Saskatoon every month for the first three or four years of Tracy's life, mostly for seizure control.

After Tracy died, various friends of the Latimers spoke up on Robert's behalf.

Psychiatrist Dr. R. P. Menzies, who had previously done psychiatric evaluations and testified as an expert witness at approximately 100 trials (for both prosecution and defence), interviewed Latimer over a period of four days for a total of nine and a half hours. Menzies described Latimer in this way:

He struck me as being a candid individual, a responsible individual, he thought about things seriously before he acted, he wasn't impulsive, he wasn't prone to angry behaviour, sort of salt of the earth type of person. I think he's a fairly stubborn individual, I think he's single-minded . . . I didn't detect any significant problem in his mental state at all . . .

In his sentencing judgment in Latimer's second trial Justice G.E. Noble wrote:

In summary the evidence establishes he is a caring and responsible person and that his relationship with Tracy was that of a loving and protective parent. On the evidence it is difficult to believe that there is anything about Mr. Latimer that could be called sinister or malevolent or even unkind towards other people.

When asked about the quality of care Tracy was getting from her parents, their family doctor, Dr. D.R. Kemp said:

I thought it was excellent.

Perhaps most telling was a comment written in dissent to the decision of the Saskatchewan Court of Appeals, in the appeal of the first trial, by Justice E.D. Bayda, the Chief Justice of Saskatchewan. Bayda, who had known Latimer for about 20 years, wrote:

The appellant is a devoted family man, devoted to his wife and his children. He is a loving, caring, nurturing person who actively participated in the daily care of the children and in particular the caring and nurturing of Tracy . . .

. . . [Robert] often bathed Tracy, fed her, cleaned up her vomit, changed her wet and dirty diapers and generally helped care for Tracy.

[Latimer] has no criminal record. He poses no risk to society and requires no rehabilitation. He enjoys a very healthy and wholesome reputation in the community . . . While the killing was a purposeful one, it had its genesis in altruism and was motivated by love, mercy and compassion or a combination of those virtues, generally considered by people to be life-enhancing and affirmative.

This informed and compassionate statement from a highly distinguished judge who not only knew Latimer but had looked extensively into this case was extraordinary.

Clearly Latimer is a good man, a man without malice, a man who does not fit the category of murderer, except as it is described in the *Criminal*

Code of Canada. Therein lies the dilemma faced by the jury: here we have a man who is clearly in violation of the law, who by the letter of the law has committed murder, but how can we possibly convict him of murder?

Brayford was in a very difficult position. What could he say in defence of Latimer? His best shot by far would have been to make a case similar to that made by Morris Manning in the Morgentaler case, as noted above ("... *it is up to you and you alone to apply the law to this evidence and you have a right to say it shouldn't be applied*") except that Chief Justice Dickson of the Supreme Court had expressly prohibited such a defence.

Necessity too was ruled out as a legitimate defence by the judges in the Latimer trials just as in the Morgentaler trials; it was deemed not in accord with case law (legal principles that emerge from past cases). Necessity is an accepted defence in some cases, but its acceptability is very limited.

Necessity could be a legitimate reason to break the letter of the law in certain cases, but it can be used only rarely, such as in a circumstance where someone is about to kill you if you don't kill them first. Claude-Armand Sheppard was able to get some traction with this idea in Morgentaler's Quebec trials, mainly because of the prosecution bringing forth witnesses like Verona Parkinson, for whom there was convincing evidence of the need for an abortion. In the Ontario trial of Morgentaler, Morris Manning was handicapped by the different charge of conspiracy, which did not call for identifying specific cases of abortion where the defence could then demonstrate need. Still Manning pleaded necessity, but his trump card was nullification. It would have been Brayford's trump card too, if he had been allowed to use it.

So Brayford dutifully proceeded with a defence of necessity, as Sheppard and Manning had done, but without the trump card to back it up. All he could hope for was that the jury, in hearing the case for necessity, might grow more sympathetic with his client. Justice Noble, presiding over this trial, was reluctant to allow Brayford to use this defence, but did agree to at least hear it and then decide if he would allow it. This put Brayford in a difficult position, but not having much else, he decided to go with it. Then after Brayford made his case to the jury, Noble told them he would not allow it after all.

There was a subtext of nullification running through all of this, not with the jury members, who could not be told about the possibility, but with Brayford, Judge Noble, and Prosecutor Neufeld. Brayford would do what he could to make the jury sympathetic without mentioning the forbidden topic. Noble and Neufeld would do everything they could to steer the jury away from thinking about nullification. Both sides were aware of what had happened in the Morgentaler trials.

Noble's odd indecision about the necessity defence was probably due to his worrying about how it had been successfully used as a pretext in the Morgentaler trials. Then when he denied it, after Brayford had used it, he probably thought it was somehow too suggestive of nullification — too supportive of the idea that Latimer had to do what he had to do, too likely to lead to juror sympathy, even if not a good legal argument.

Brayford did everything he could get away with to encourage sympathy for his client. He even used Latimer's legal naiveté as indication of Latimer's sincerity and honesty. He quoted from a televised interview Latimer had given to the CBC before the trials started. Latimer said:

I don't necessarily agree with Mark Brayford's way of handling this, but in the end I do, because I am totally lost in these matters, and you have to go with the lawyer, basically, when you're in court.

Brayford argued that this "fish out of the water" aspect of Latimer was apparent in his dealings with the law, as in not getting a lawyer at first and then publicly questioning Brayford's strategy. Brayford was painting a picture of an innocent thrown into a situation he was not well equipped to handle. This is not a criminal, Brayford was in effect telling the jury, but a good and honest man who simply did what his daughter desperately needed him to do, whatever the consequences.

Coming perilously close to the forbidden topic, he said that they, the jury, could decide what constituted necessity. That is probably what then prompted Noble to throw the defence out. If the jury could decide what necessity was, then it could have a pretext for a verdict of not guilty. Noble could not let them go down that road, for there lay nullification.

No one was sure where the jury stood when it went out for deliberations. It was clear that Latimer had broken the law and his main defence had been disallowed. But a compelling case for sympathy had emerged. Did the jury members understand that they could nullify? If so, were they sympathetic enough to do so?

The first insight into the jury's thinking occurred when the jury came back with a question for Judge Noble:

> *Is there any possible way we can have input into a recommendation for sentencing?*

This was a highly revealing question. Clearly there was reluctance to find Latimer guilty, and concern that, if they did find him so, the penalty would be too severe.

Yikes, Noble must have thought to himself. Nullification must be brewing! What he did next was crucial to the outcome of the trial. He told them that they should just concern themselves with guilt or innocence and not be influenced by the penalty. That is a standard judicial point of view, directing juries away from considerations that might cause, for example, undue sympathy for the defendant. That would have been exactly Noble's concern, because there too lies nullification. Since that was a standard judicial response, it can be forgiven, but what he said next is not and cannot:

> *. . . later on, once you have reached a verdict, you — we will have some discussions about that, but not at this stage of the game.*

This may have been a momentary misstep, but it had a profound effect on the outcome of the trial. Clearly the jury was expressing some level of sympathy with Latimer. Had Noble been more straightforward in his response here, telling the jury the truth that there was a ten-year minimum sentence for second-degree murder, and that any negotiations on the length of sentence would take place from that base of ten years, he might well have had a jury refusing to convict.

Why was Noble so concerned about this? It was not that he was against Latimer; some of his later actions, including his statement about Latimer quoted earlier, show that he, like the jury, was sympathetic. But Noble, like most judges, like Chief Justice Dickson, hated the idea of nullification. These are people with a lifetime invested in supporting the legal system, in believing in the absolute rule of law, and in directing juries to follow the law. They have built up in their minds a deep antipathy to the idea, an antipathy that does not, in my mind, stand up to close scrutiny (see Chapters 7 and 8). Noble was not hostile to Latimer, but he was very much against jury nullification.

Noble did not take much time to deliberate over his statement that "we will have some discussions," and might have thought better of it if he had. As it turned out, it seemed like an intentional and disingenuous attempt, and a successful one, to lead the jury away from nullification. The jury took his statement to mean that punishment for Latimer could be moderated, that even if found guilty of murder he would not be treated like Clifford Olson or Paul Bernardo.

With the jury out of the room, Brayford pleaded with Noble to come clean with the jury and tell them about the ten-year minimum. This was, after all, public knowledge that apparently none of the jury members happened to know. Was it right to withhold such public information? Was it fair that another jury in a similar case might well include someone who knew about the minimum sentence and that jury, knowing this, would refuse to find the defendant guilty? Is this equal justice under the law? But Noble was firm in rejecting Brayford's plea to be forthcoming with the jury.

After four hours of deliberation the jury came back with a verdict of guilty. Laura, sitting just behind her husband, screamed, "No, no, no, no!"

Latimer turned to her and hugged her, saying: "It's okay. It's okay."

When a shaken and bitter Latimer was leaving the courthouse he said, "I thought I'd get at least one vote, but I guess not."

But he almost surely had one vote, and maybe twelve. The jury had been tricked into thinking it could get a light sentence for him. It had been tricked into moving away from nullification. The ten-year incarceration minimum that resulted for Latimer was not as severe as the sentences of malicious child-killers Bernardo and Olson, but it was roughly the same length as that of Bernardo's co-offender, Karla Homolka. And Latimer is on parole for life, while Homolka has been entirely free for years now.

The jury was stunned when it heard, shortly after their verdict had been announced, that there was a ten-year minimum incarceration for second-degree murder, which is what they had just pinned on Latimer. Some gasped, some put their hands to their mouths; a few cried.

But the damage had been done; once their verdict was announced they lost all real power. They had held power, the power to nullify, but that was gone now, and they probably never even understood that they had it: thanks to Chief Justice Dickson it was a secret that no one, not even the defence lawyer, could mention to them.

The jury made one last attempt to moderate the sentence, making a plea for a one-year token sentence; whatever the law said, they argued, one year would be much more appropriate in this case. Noble, to his credit, thought about it for a month and then did try to fulfill the jury's wishes. He too must have realized the unfairness of the trial outcome. Noble did pass the sentence of one year, arguing this on the basis of what is called a "Constitutional exemption" to the mandatory sentence. The *Charter of Rights and Freedoms* forbids "cruel and unusual punishment," and Noble argued that in this case the mandatory minimum would be cruel and unusual. But he probably knew it would not fly.

Appeal courts are reluctant to accept the circumvention of mandatory minimums, arguing that these were the expressed will of legislators and the judiciary ought to respect that. The Saskatchewan Court of Appeals overturned Noble's sentencing decision and imposed the ten-year minimum. Subsequently the Supreme Court of Canada also upheld that minimum and rejected other appeals from Latimer's lawyers, who by this time included the eminent Toronto defence lawyer Edward Greenspan.

The court also ruled that Noble was right not to tell the jury about the mandatory minimum and that "the trial did not become unfair simply because the trial judge undermined the jury's de facto power to nullify."

But was it fair? Can any neutral person stand back from this and call it fair? If Noble had not made the misleading statement about sentencing, Latimer might well have been found not guilty. And had Chief Justice Dickson not turned the whole idea of nullification into a dark secret — a topic forbidden from discussion in court — is it not likely that a Brayford address to the jury, like Manning's address in the last Morgentaler trial, might well have won the day with a similarly sympathetic jury?

In 2009 I asked Mark Brayford about all of this. He said:

> *I just could not believe how the best justice system in the world could end up with such a wrong result . . . Worst of all, the chance of such terrible unfairness repeating itself is increasing rather than decreasing.*

I asked him why he said it was increasing, and he answered:

> *Historically, the greatest safeguard against unfair laws has been the power of juries to refuse to convict if it would be unfair to apply the law to a particular case. In my view, juries should be instructed that, if at all possible, they should apply the law as written, unless they are unanimously sure that it would be unjust to do so.*

*Since the Supreme Court decided Dr. Morgentaler's appeal, you
dare not hint that a jury exercise this fundamental and proper
power that they possess. Jury nullification still existed after
Morgentaler, but you dared not tell the jury of their power after
what the Supreme Court said to counsel in that case, that Mr.
Manning was quite simply wrong to say to the jury that if they
did not like the law they need not enforce it. [According to the
Court] he should not have done so. The Latimer Case undermines
this important power even further when the Court states that the
trial did not become unfair simply because the trial judge
undermined the jury's de facto power to nullify. Arguably, since
Robert Latimer's case, judges can even say things to a jury to try
to prevent them from exercising this function.*

Brayford could have added that even a misleading statement by the
presiding judge, leading the jury away from nullification, is allowed. For
more on Mark Brayford's comments see Chapter Notes.

Dickson in his 1988 ruling has succeeded in turning the power of
jury nullification into a secret kept from juries. Has this made Canadian
courts more fair? I am sure Robert Latimer does not think so. Nor, I
suspect, do his jurors. Nor do many Canadians who are concerned about
justice in our courts.

CHAPTER 7

THE CASE FOR JURY INDEPENDENCE

Most critics of nullification acknowledge that we cannot abolish jury independence and a jury's power to nullify (or to use Justice Dickson's phrase, a jury's "de facto discretion"). But at the same time the critics — and this includes many members of the judiciary, many lawyers, and especially prosecutors — want to suppress this power. They do this because they rightly want juries to follow the law. But some critics, like Chief Justice Dickson, go too far in this: they want to keep jury independence and nullification a secret.

Keeping knowledge a secret is almost the same thing as banning it. Most juries will not know that they have the option of refusing to follow the letter of the law, and if they do have some vague idea that they might be able to do so, and they have an inclination to do so, they will likely be intimidated and steered away from it by stern (and, as we have seen in the Latimer case, sometimes misleading) directions from the judge.

Note: knowledge about the power to nullify is not the only thing that is kept secret in courts — some other secrets are mentioned in Chapter Notes.

The Canadian judiciary, led by Dickson's ruling, is trying to have it both ways. The judiciary knows that jury independence is a long-standing and fundamental principle of English law; *that* cannot be denied. At the same time they stack the deck so strongly against nullification that one wonders if, under present conditions, it will ever happen in Canadian courts again. Essentially our judges say that in theory we accept the idea, but in practice we will do everything we can to make sure it does not happen.

In practice we no longer really have jury independence. Why should we care about this? The Morgentaler and Latimer cases were presented here to show why it matters, and in this chapter I will elaborate on the reasons why we might lament what we have lost, or at least mostly lost, in our legal system.

PROTECTION OF THE INNOCENT

English-based legal systems place a high value on protection of the innocent. The idea that authorities might punish someone unjustly is abhorrent to us. And so it should be: if the state can arbitrarily and unfairly punish anyone, none of us is safe. And just as we do not want the innocent punished, we do not want punishment of the guilty to be out of proportion to the crime: no crime, no punishment; modest crime, modest punishment. As Gilbert and Sullivan's Mikado advised, "Let the punishment fit the crime."

We have developed all sorts of legal devices to protect us from over-zealous police and prosecutors. Arrests must follow certain protocols: formal charges, subject to judicial override, are usually required for detention; in prosecution there is a presumption of innocence; there are strict rules for the admissibility of evidence; and the accused are entitled to legal counsel. All these are in the service of fairness to the accused and protection of the innocent.

Our commitment to this comes, in part, from the great English legal writer William Blackstone, who wrote the highly influential

Commentaries on the Laws of England in the mid-eighteenth century. Many of Blackstone's ideas not only influenced British law but played a prominent role in the development of the legal systems in Canada and the United States.

Perhaps the most famous of Blackstone's ideas became known as Blackstone's Formulation:

> *It is better that ten guilty go free than one innocent be punished.*

This great expression of human rights is not, of course, meant to be taken literally. Blackstone's Formulation simply tells us that it is a greater failing of our justice system when an innocent person is dealt with unfairly than when a criminal goes free. This sensibility is sometimes contrasted with a different formulation attributed to Bismarck:

> *It is better that ten innocents be punished than one guilty go free.*

Is it the spirit of Blackstone that we want to guide our legal system, or is it the spirit of Bismarck? If it is the former then we should welcome the existence of a final check, by peers of the accused, of not only the general efficacy of a law but the justice of applying a law in particular circumstances. We should welcome any device that might protect us from unjust results.

The law is too blunt an instrument to always protect the innocent, or to avert punishment that does not fit the crime. That is why the spirit of Blackstone would seem to demand that we openly countenance jury nullification.

The *Criminal Code* was not designed for, nor does it well serve, cases like that of Robert Latimer. Nor was it designed for cases like that of Henry Morgentaler. We have seen, though, why Morgentaler's worked out well, and why Latimer's did not.

In Morgentaler's case the law, through the intervention of juries, functioned as though it were guided by the spirit of William Blackstone and his formulation. In Latimer's case, because the presiding judge blocked an intervention by his jury, he was convicted and punished as a murderer.

* * *

In light of Blackstone's Formulation, let us look back at the examples of nullification cited in the first two chapters. The positive examples of nullification, such as Penn, Zenger, Morgentaler, and Jenkins all foreshadowed dramatic and positive social changes. Some of them (Bates, Krieger, Pritchard and Olditch, Nanavati) reflected public sympathy and distaste for overly severe punishment. Jury nullification brought a welcome voice of mercy to these justice systems. The cases where the outcomes were not positive — the trials for the murder of the Donnellys, Emmett Till, and the trial of O.J. Simpson (if we count that as an example of nullification) — did not result in significant social change for the worse. In fact, the Till case energized the civil rights movement. The downside was that a few culpable people went free.

It was outrageous that Till's murderers escaped prison sentences, but did it really, in the long run, matter very much? This refusal to convict did not result in more lynching; rather, by bringing the pervasive bigotry of the American South into open public scrutiny it helped bring about positive social change. The murderers Bryant and Milam were spared prison, but after the trial they led miserable lives anyway. And so what if they *had* led relatively normal lives, or if the Donnelly killers did so? The glare of publicity likely meant they would not, any of them, kill again. And none of the above got off entirely free: they all had to live with their consciences, such as those consciences were. And if they had no consciences, then more the pity for their barren lives.

The point here is the huge imbalance between the consequences of the positive cases and the negative ones. We live in a significantly better world today because of the courage of some juries to stand up against unjust laws. And we do not live in a significantly worse one because some juries allowed a few killers to go free.

There are undoubtedly cases where nullification has led to some social harm; like any principle of law it can at times go seriously awry. But it is easier to imagine such abuses, as Chief Justice Dickson does, than to find actual cases. And even if one can be cited, we do not abandon a valued principle of law every time it is abused. If we did that, we would be left with no principles at all.

PROTECTION AGAINST ARBITRARY PROSECUTION

The idea of a panel of peers being responsible for verdicts in criminal prosecutions was adopted in Magna Carta because it was a way of protecting individuals against arbitrary punishment by authorities, as discussed in Chapter 3. This possibility of too harshly punishing citizens remains all-too-real today, as the Latimer case clearly demonstrated.

If juries are going to serve their original purpose of protecting citizens against arbitrary authority, then they must themselves, in rendering verdicts, be free of all external authority — political, judicial, and legal. This is obvious when it comes to influence from politicians, but it is also true when it comes to the influence of judges who can be co-opted to serve political interests (as when the 2000 American presidential election was stolen for George W. Bush by the American Supreme Court). If juries are going to be impartial voices seeking justice in the face of political influence, then they must stand independent of judges when it comes to reaching a verdict.

In rendering verdicts they must be independent of the authority of laws as well. Juries, in order to fully play their role in being independent voices of justice and standing up against arbitrary punishment by authorities, must be not only free of politicians and judges in reaching their verdicts; it follows that they must also be free of the letter of the law. Laws are made by politicians (and by judges in case law), and if those laws are viewed as sacrosanct, then they become another way of imposing unfair and arbitrary punishment.

PUNISHING JURIES?

Suppose that we did try to ensure that juries followed the letter of the law — suppose we decided that universal respect for the law is more important than jury independence. How would that work? How would recalcitrant jurors be punished? Would there be jail sentences or fines if a jury did not come in with a verdict that was in accord with what the judge saw as the legally correct verdict?

Such an eventuality would completely undermine the jury system as it currently works. The dynamics of a trial would change drastically, as the defence lawyer and the prosecutor would simply forget about the jury and address the judge, who would now have all the power in the proceedings. And who would want to sit on such a jury, with no power and subject to some sort of punishment if they came to the wrong verdict?

How could jurors have any semblance of disinterested assessment of the facts in a case? Instead they would be preoccupied with coming up with a verdict that suited the judge, in order to avoid whatever punishment was in place to ensure compliance with the law.

What would be the point of juries at all, if the judge can simply invoke the law and tell them what they must do? Why not save a lot of time and money and do away with juries completely?

It is easy to see that juries, if they are going to have any real value, cannot be obliged to come to any particular verdict.

A DOUBLE STANDARD: PROSECUTORIAL AND JUDICIAL NULLIFICATION OF THE LAW

A jury is not the only trial participant with the power to nullify the law. Prosecutorial nullification, unquestioned in legal circles, arises much more often than does jury nullification. Such action by juries is a rare occurrence. With prosecutors, on the other hand, it happens virtually every day.

THE CASE FOR JURY INDEPENDENCE

Suppose a prosecutor is dealing with a case of murder. First-degree murder is defined in Canada as causing the death of another person in a planned or deliberate manner. Second-degree murder is causing death in, say, a fight where there was no explicit plan to cause death, although there was an intention to cause bodily harm. Manslaughter is defined in the *Criminal Code of Canada* to be causing death while carrying out an illegal act, but without the intention of causing bodily harm.

Suppose the prosecutor feels that a charge of either first- or second-degree murder, with attendant mandatory minimum sentences, is too harsh, even though according to the *Criminal Code* murder is without question the correct charge. That prosecutor could decide to press a lesser charge, say manslaughter, thereby unilaterally determining that application of the letter of the law would be inappropriate in this particular case. Is that not nullification? It happens all the time, without so much as a squawk from most quarters. Jury nullification, on the other hand, elicits many squawks from many quarters, including the Supreme Court of Canada.

It is a good thing that our courts allow a certain degree of such prosecutorial discretion in pressing charges — discretion often used in cases like mercy killing or other cases where the defendant clearly broke the law but the prosecutor feels murder is too severe a charge, with too inflexible a penalty. A first-degree murder conviction entails a minimum twenty-five years of incarceration, a second-degree conviction, ten. For a manslaughter conviction, the sentence is at the judge's discretion.

In 2006, eighty-three-year-old Edmontonian Noel Lavery was charged with and convicted of manslaughter for smothering his alcoholic wife who, he claimed, was "at death's door." Although he was tempted to press a charge of murder, prosecutor Mark Huyser-Wierenga chose manslaughter.

In 1997, Ronald Leonard Brown was charged with manslaughter for having smothered severely disabled eleven-year-old Ronald Lambert to death, twenty years earlier. He was given two years. There are many other such cases of prosecutors deciding, because of circumstances, to bypass the letter of the law and reduce charges.

Prosecutors can nullify the law in two ways. One is when they decide, based upon extenuating circumstances as in the cases above, to press a charge that is less than that directed by the law. This includes deciding not to press a charge at all if they believe there is not a substantial likelihood of a conviction, or if they simply decide it is not in the public interest to pursue the case.

The second kind of prosecutorial nullification is called plea bargaining: bargaining a charge down in return for an admission of guilt or some such concession. In 1992, Toronto nurse Scott Mataya was originally charged with first-degree murder for administering a lethal dose of potassium chloride to a terminally ill patient who had had his ventilator removed and was expected to die within an hour. Mataya was distressed when the patient started to choke, and administered the potassium chloride, which caused death in minutes. The charge was reduced to administering a noxious substance when Mataya agreed to plead guilty to this lesser charge.

Judges also nullify the law, although they, like prosecutors, do not call it that. When hearing a case without a jury, judges can simply dismiss a case, saying simply that they are "not persuaded by the evidence," which might or might not be the case. In some instances, where they can see no purpose in convicting a defendant for whom there is persuasive evidence of guilt, they will simply decide not to convict, much like a jury does when it nullifies the law. Judges will often nullify the law in this way in cases involving spousal battery, where pre-emptive murder of an abusive husband, while not recognized as a defence by the *Criminal Code*, has been accepted by judges as a legitimate defence.

It can also be argued that judges, if not nullifying the law, do modify the law whenever they set a precedent. Case law (or common law) involves citing of precedents, which is often done in a selective manner so as to push the verdict in a direction favoured by the judge.

Why then, we might ask, is there so much opposition to juries nullifying the law — so much so that the Supreme Court forbids mentioning it in court? Why, when it is done frequently by prosecutors and judges? Is it because we do not usually refer to it as nullification when prosecutors or judges do it? Then we call it prosecutorial or judicial discretion. Jury nullification, on the other hand, sounds like something bad, some flouting of the law carried out by racists in the American South.

Is this double standard acceptable because we can trust prosecutors and judges, but not juries, with this power? What about the prosecutors like Robichaud in the Morgentaler case and Kirkham in the Latimer case?

Just asking.

THE FEELINGS OF HUMANITY

The law must be about something more than legal calculation. In 1765 William Blackstone wrote:

> *Mankind will not be reasoned out of the feelings of humanity.*

Blackstone was a man of exceptional reasoning abilities, which is partly why the legal arguments he constructed in his famous eighteenth-century work *Commentaries on English Law* were so influential. But the power of his work came from more than his incisive reasoning; it also came from his expression of human dignity and his respect for the "feelings of humanity" that put a human face on the law.

For Blackstone, justice was not simply about laws; it was about what was right. Courts found strong legal reasons to find Henry Morgentaler guilty, but his juries, charged with making the final decision, could not accept that such a decision was right. The court could not reason them out of their feelings of humanity.

Juries, if properly instructed, will understand the importance of respecting the law, but they should also understand that it is within their powers to stand up against the law when application of that law would be an affront to the feelings of humanity, when a verdict of guilty would be an assault upon their consciences.

With due respect given to the law, jurors convinced that a particular verdict is wrong should not be asked or expected to vote against their consciences. We should not want them to. We should be glad that our system of law enforcement allows this final, human check on the justice of the law.

CONSTITUTIONAL ARGUMENTS

Section 11(f) of the Canadian Charter of Rights and Freedoms reads:

> *Any person charged with an offence has the right, except in cases of an offence under military law tried before a military tribunal, to the benefit of a trial by jury where the punishment for the offence is imprisonment for five years or a more severe punishment.*

What is the "benefit of a trial by jury" if not some advantage to the accused in a jury, rather than a judge, giving the verdict? It is not that a jury will be more knowledgeable or capable in any respect; juries are lay people with no likely expertise in the law. So what is the benefit the constitution speaks of?

If we are citing the "benefit of trial by jury," we are citing some benefit that extends beyond knowledge of the law. As Christopher Nowlin wrote in 2007–08 in the *Criminal Law Quarterly* "the critical difference between the function of a judge and a jury is that only a jury can lawfully disregard substantive law, and will do so occasionally on the basis of community standards."

Nowlin goes on to argue that the role commonly assigned by judges to the jury, to simply determine the facts, would not be one that would confer "benefit" upon the accused. Jury members as lay people are not as likely to be as skilled in deducing facts from evidence as are people trained in the law and experienced in assessing evidence from witnesses.

The only real benefit of a jury would come in their ability to act against the law — to nullify the law.

But there can be no "benefit" from the ability to "lawfully disregard substantive law" if juries do not know they can do that. In blocking nullification, Chief Justice Dickson has blocked this benefit of juries, which is clearly contrary to the intent of the *Charter*.

* * *

There is another *Charter* clause that supports informing juries of their right to nullify. Section 15 (1) states that:

> *Every individual is equal before and under the law and has the right to equal protection and equal benefit of the law without discrimination . . .*

Under Justice Dickson's ruling, which prohibits mentioning a jury's power to nullify, some juries will happen to know about this power, because one or more members will know about it, while other juries will simply not know. Hiding this power from juries results in discrimination against certain defendants: those unlucky enough to have juries that do not know the secret. Defendants that do have juries who know about nullification will have a possibility of a not-guilty verdict that is unavailable to those with less-informed juries.

That is unequal protection under the law. Again, Dickson's proclamation on jury nullification appears to have been contrary to the intent of the *Charter*.

CIVIL LIBERTIES

There are real questions here in regard to civil liberties. Is Dickson's prohibition on speaking to juries about their actual rights a violation of the basic civil liberty of freedom of speech? In Section 2(b) the *Charter* guarantees freedom of expression, but the idea long predates the *Charter*. Free speech is a long-established principle of western democracies.

There are, of course, certain exceptions to the rule — yelling fire on a crowded theatre, to use the most common example. And in special cases like juries it is reasonable that the information given to jury members is somewhat limited so that they will not be unduly influenced by the media or by any other external sources. But how can it be right to bar defence lawyers from informing juries of their fundamental right to nullify the law? That seems to violate the standard of free discourse that we value so highly.

Most judges, of course, including Justice Noble, do not want juries to nullify; they want juries to play the narrower role of determining facts. But that is not up to them to decide. Judges are fully within their rights to urge juries to follow the law, but they cannot compel them to do so and ought not to be able to withhold any crucial information that would allow them to make a better-informed decision. This includes information about the power to nullify and other points that might be relevant to nullification such as mandatory minimum sentences. For more on sentencing see "Other Secrets" in Chapter Notes.

Forbidding access to knowledge in any activity ought to be well justified. The *Charter* protection of this basic civil liberty of freedom of expression is not absolute, but there should be very good reasons for any sort of censorship or hiding of knowledge

Moreover, information about nullification and sentencing is publicly and very readily available. Members of some juries would have known about the power to nullify as well as the minimum sentence for second-degree murder, while others like Latimer's did not know. It is unfair to the defendant, and discriminatory, that some juries have these crucial bits of information and others do not. Again it seems to be a violation of the intention of the *Charter*.

One last point should be made about civil liberties. An important principle of law, and another way we try to protect the innocent, is that a defendant should be able to present his or her best possible defence. (See Chapter Notes for a discussion of what constitutes a defence.) In the Latimer case, for example, his only real defence would have been similar to the one Morris Manning used to defend Morgentaler: yes, of course he may be technically guilty, but it would be wrong to convict him, given the inordinately severe punishment that would result from conviction. If authorities can prohibit a defendant's best defence, then such defendants are once again, as they were before juries were established, subject to arbitrary punishment by authorities.

MERCY

In Western culture, highly influenced by Christian thought, there may be no higher virtue than that of mercy. We love the idea; it warms our hearts. It makes us feel good about human nature that we care for one another and that we are kind and merciful beings.

Except in practice we mostly are not. We, and often the most ostensibly devout Christians among us, are much too often unforgiving and filled with thoughts of revenge and vindictiveness rather than mercy.

It is partly the law that makes us so. We believe in the law and respect its importance in a civilized society, but at the same time it is a blunt instrument of justice. It really leaves too little room for society to be merciful. Guilt is guilt, according to the law, and the law is the law. Prosecutors do have some leeway, as discussed earlier, in moderating charges brought against defendants. And judges, when they are not limited by mandatory minimum sentencing rules, have some opportunity to show mercy, such as by dismissing a case or in handing down a lesser sentence. There is also the device of "diversion" whereby prosecutors can allow certain first-time offenders who admit their guilt to escape going to trial, perhaps giving them some hours of community service. There is also developing interest in the idea of restorative justice, whereby the guilty party can work to atone for his or her crime, rather than simply being punished in the way directed by the law. But there is not much in the justice system that provides for the extending of a merciful hand. It just does not fit with the way the system works, most of the time.

Defences based on an appeal for jury nullification are perhaps the most significant way the courts can exercise mercy. In my book on the Latimer case I gave an example of what his defence lawyer might have been able to say in his closing remarks to the jury, had not the Dickson ruling against mentioning nullification not been in place. It concluded:

> *The Bible says, "blessed are the merciful, for they shall obtain mercy." Sadly, in this world at least, such is not always the case. But you [the jury members] have an opportunity to see that, in this case at least, the merciful does receive mercy. It is up to you to make that decision, and I implore you to do so.*

Such a comment, or anything like it alluding to the possibility of jury nullification, was forbidden by Justice Dickson's ruling.

If we are to be true to our commitment to mercy, then we must preserve and protect jury independence. It allows for the possibility of humane, merciful intervention in the highly structured and somewhat inflexible process of the administration of justice.

CONCLUDING COMMENTS

In this section I have presented reasons why jury independence and jury nullification are important aspects of our legal system and ought not to be kept so secret. As mentioned above, hiding these ideas is similar, in effect, to banning them. Hiding and banning are, in practice, almost the same thing. Neither should be acceptable to us.

I should qualify that. What if there is something so terrible about jury nullification that even if we cannot abolish it we should just keep it quiet lest some jury actually nullify? I cannot think of any parallel bit of knowledge that fits that description, but let us allow for the moment that these matters — jury independence and nullification — are so dangerous that juries should not be informed about them. What are the arguments in favour of suppressing this knowledge? I have touched on them briefly in looking at Justice Dickson's reasons for banning talking about nullification in court. In the next chapter I critically review all the main reasons given in support of Dickson's position.

Are these reasons sufficient to override the reasons I have given in this chapter for an open approach to jury independence and nullification?

You be the judge.

CHAPTER 8

EXAMINING THE ARGUMENTS AGAINST JURY INDEPENDENCE

I see no justification for, and considerable harm in, this deliberate lack of candor.

David L. Bazelon, Chief Judge,
US Court of Appeals, DC (1972), writing in reference to jury rights

JUSTICE VS. THE RULE OF THE MAJORITY

In the Western world, democracy is widely seen to be a flawed but essential approach to governing a society. As Churchill said, it is "the worst form of government, except for all the others." We incorporate democratic principles, especially rule by majority, in all sorts of public and private activities. Democratic nations will have votes on matters of national importance, but the idea is so entrenched that we are also inclined to call for a vote whenever there is a choice to be made on anything. Book clubs will vote on which book to read for their next meeting. Differences with as few as three people involved are settled by determining the will of the majority. Even children in playgrounds do this.

I recall that in the anti-authoritarian years of the 1960s and '70s the idea of voting on everything became even more prevalent. Radical university students would stage protests and insist that their institutions were undemocratic because the majority of people there — the students — were not allowed to choose the curriculum they would study. I remember when I was a young faculty member being confronted by students who demanded to know if our institution was a democracy or not. It was not a question to which one could easily give a winning answer. An answer of "No, we are not a democracy," would be greeted by howls of outrage and charges of being a fascist. Agreeing that we should be a democracy, on the other hand, would have meant young people who had no idea what, say, sociology was would be determining the reading list for courses in that discipline. Some teachers agreed to give up that authority (and, if I remember correctly, many of them did happen to be sociologists) while others of us just put up with bearing the title of fascists.

Should we be ruled by the will of the majority in all things? In a democracy our laws are drawn up by legislatures consisting of our duly elected representatives. Is it ever right to refuse to abide by those laws?

The most basic and most frequent objection to jury nullification is that it takes the right to make laws out of the hands of elected legislators and gives that right over to a random group of citizens on a jury. Jury nullification, then, is seen as being undemocratic.

But such a view is taking the idea of democracy and rule by majority too far. Alexis de Tocqueville saw this problem long ago when he visited the young American republic in 1831 and wrote his classic work, *Democracy in America*. Tocqueville wrote about the "tyranny of the majority," by which he meant the unchallenged power created by allegiance to the idea of rule by majority. He feared any sort of unchecked power. Rule by majority is an idea, he writes, based upon the belief that better ideas come from an assembly of people than from an individual. He could have gone further: rule by majority is based on the belief that fifty per cent plus one more person is wiser than fifty per cent minus one person. All power is given to the first, none to the second.

This power of the majority becomes especially problematic when it comes to broader areas of human concern, such as justice. Is justice the same as the decision of the majority? Or, in other words, is justice the same as the consequences of applying the law? Clearly not, in certain instances. We accept laws devised by legislatures because there is no better alternative — we do not want to return to the idea of rule of individuals rather than laws, and how can we make laws other than by the will of the majority? But we should be under no illusion that our laws obtained democratically are an infallible guide to justice.

What can we do, then, when the law is in conflict with justice? We can just let it be so, and say that is the necessary consequence of rule by law. This is the position of those who make the democratic argument against jury nullification: the law is the law and no one but democratically elected representatives should be able to change that law.

This is, I believe, an expression of the tyranny Tocqueville was referring to. The law might be wrong or unfair but it is the law determined by the majority, and it shall remain supreme.

Can we really be comfortable, though, with such a bald assertion about the law? Should Henry Morgentaler simply have left the needs of desperate women unattended, because the law said he should? Should we not worry when a man like Robert Latimer, who has committed an act of mercy, is punished as severely as a malicious killer? Are these injustices simply the price we pay for democracy and rule by majority?

Given that we generally accept the failings of democracy because other possibilities seem worse, there are a few things we can do to seek justice in the face of legally sanctioned injustice. Perhaps most obviously we can campaign for the election of those who we believe represent a greater commitment to justice, and hope that such people can become the majority and change offending laws. That is what many critics of jury nullification urge: if you do not like the law, they say, then change it through the ballot box. Often this is presented as an argument-clincher in discussions of nullification.

This is, however, a facile position of very limited application. First, finding political candidates to support one's position on changing the law would be difficult enough, but there are always many issues to evaluate in a candidate. One presumably votes on the basis of an overall assessment of all the candidate's views, not just one. So it would be fortunate indeed to find someone who was not only willing to fight for a change in a particular law but who also had the best overall combination of positions, as well as having personal qualities one admired.

Second, the process of changing the law, even if one could find some political traction for the idea, is very cumbersome, and is extremely unlikely to happen in a fashion timely enough to help the defendant for whom the issue may have arisen. Third, the problem is not always with who has written the laws but with the inflexibility of laws. It is impossible to write laws that cover all eventualities; possible injustices will arise no matter how enlightened the lawmakers. Fourth, abandoning the possibility of the remedy of jury nullification in favour of seeking political change loses the many benefits of independent juries discussed earlier, benefits that are constitutionally guaranteed.

This ballot box solution to society's ills is a long-term matter, and is vastly overrated by those who see it as a practical means of dealing with immediate examples of social injustice.

Another action we can take against a perceived injustice is to engage in acts of civil disobedience. For example, if our elected representatives continue to ignore global warming, or engage in other acts of environmental abuse that are a violation of our individual consciences, then we have a moral justification for defying the law. Such defiance is morally defensible only if one does so in full acceptance of submitting to the legally designated punishment for such offences. Otherwise acts of civil disobedience are indistinguishable from mere lawlessness, which cannot, in the interests of the greater good, be socially condoned. Though often condemned by authorities, a genuine and legitimate act of civil disobedience is an honourable way for ordinary citizens to fight back against the tyranny of the majority.

Yet another way we can fight back against the tyranny of the majority and unjust laws is the subject of this book: jury nullification. This is not a form of civil disobedience, as it is sometimes described. It is a fully legal, constitutionally protected action available only to juries, an action that can provide ordinary citizens sitting on a jury with the power to redress a legal injustice.

Jury nullification runs counter to the democratic impulse of many who decry its existence. But, for the reasons discussed in the previous chapter, jury independence is a cornerstone of our legal system. Independence is necessary for juries to have any real purpose or to offer any real benefit to the accused. It is a legitimate and essential counter to the excesses of democracy: it allows for justice, which ought to be our highest goal, to override the will of the majority.

Tocqueville wrote:

> When I refuse to obey an unjust law, I by no means deny the majority's right to give orders; I only appeal from the sovereignty of the people to the sovereignty of the human race.

An independent jury is a legal way, a way beyond the commands of the majority, to appeal to the sovereignty of the human race — to the commands of human decency and justice.

PRESERVATION OF THE RULE OF LAW

This is a slightly different concern from the one above, which worries about violating the sanctity of democratically determined laws. The concern here is that if we allow juries the power to not follow the law then we are opening the floodgates of lawlessness, and anarchy will reign. Our freedom, the argument goes, depends upon clear laws to guide us.

Justice Dickson's 1988 ruling referred to this argument when he quoted a judgment in a 1784 case from Britain:

To be free is to live under government by law . . . Miserable is the
condition of individuals, dangerous is the condition of the state,
if there is no certain law, or, which is the same thing, no certain
administration of law, to protect individuals, or to guard the State.

There is no question that it is essential that laws be clear and definite, both for the sake of individuals and for the stability of the state.

But is it reasonable to think that jury nullification's very limited power to override the law, which only arises in those rare circumstances where a jury believes a guilty verdict would be unjust, is somehow going to result in widespread lawlessness?

A jury's decision to go against the law represents twelve citizens' considered judgment that there is something wrong with applying the law in a particular case. It is made after hearing evidence and then entering into group deliberations on what verdict to come to. It is not wanton or thoughtless disregard of the law; indeed, in most instances the presiding judge has urged the jury to follow the law, and made it clear what the law says. A verdict which "goes against the evidence," as lawyers put it, is a verdict which is made after due consideration by all the jurors.

Does such a verdict somehow create disrespect for the law, and therefore encourage lawlessness in that way? We need to look at two different sorts of nullification — good examples and bad ones — to consider this question.

In the instances where nullification has had what most people consider to be good outcomes, as in the Morgentaler and Zenger cases, or avoids unreasonable or pointless punishment, as in the Bates case, then surely nullification increases respect for the law. Instead of a monolithic, unsympathetic, unyielding force that insists on applying a law that ought not to be applied to the case at hand, nullification in these cases puts a human face on the law; it shows that the law has a way of finding justice when legal proceedings would otherwise lead to injustice. This brings about not disrespect for the rule of law, but renewed respect for it, because the legal system is seen to seek justice rather than rigorous insistence upon legal procedures.

But what of the instances where a jury's disregard for the law has undeniably bad consequences, as in the trials of the murderers of the Donnellys and of Emmett Till? Do such events cause disrespect for the law? It seems instead that they often galvanize support for the law. Both of these cases and others where nullification has been used to bad ends have instead caused a reaction against the social conditions that allowed for such a miscarriage of justice.

Juries are not a renegade force that, if allowed their independence, will provoke a spree of lawlessness. They are a constitutionally specified body charged both with ascertaining the facts in a trial and with rendering a verdict that is just. They increase regard for law, not decrease it. Even when making bad decisions, independent juries highlight broader social concerns, such as endemic racism, and lead to greater public awareness of those issues.

THE FAIR AND EQUAL APPLICATION OF THE LAW

The argument is this: if in every case we insist on the rigorous application of the law as it is written, then we will be treating everyone equally under the law, as the Constitution insists we do. Would it be fair, Justice Dickson asked, if in two cases being tried for the same crime, one jury nullified the law and found the defendant not guilty, while the other followed the law and found a similar defendant guilty?

This sort of thing — unfair and unequal treatment under the law — happens all the time, but not because of jury nullification. There are vast differences in the abilities of defence lawyers, meaning the wealthy can get the most renowned and successful (as in the O.J. Simpson case) and the poor are often not well-served, a problem that is exacerbated by recent cuts to legal aid in Canada. The wealthy can afford to have talented lawyers exploring every possible line of defence, while those without financial resources have to make do with limited legal assistance.

Of course, having more sources of inequality is not a good thing, but if nullification is such a source, it is a very tiny one. Such inequality would occur only when two identical cases appeared and one jury decided to nullify and the other did not. The cases would have to be identical to the extent that no other factors could be influencing the juries' decisions. Both juries would have to be equally informed, and twelve jurors in one trial would all have to vote one way and the twelve on the other vote the opposite way.

This hardly seems something to worry about.

On the other hand, the "fair and equal" clause of the Constitution is relevant here, but in a different way than imagined by Dickson. As argued earlier, a source of significant unfairness and inequality occurs when some jury members have the knowledge that they can nullify the law and others do not. This has very serious and real consequences for defendants. Morgentaler's juries knew they could nullify, and so he went free. Latimer's jury did not know, and he was imprisoned for ten years.

Dickson's prohibition on telling juries about their power to nullify means this power will be used in an inconsistent manner, depending on what jury members happen to know about it.

This is a more serious inconsistency, in this case stemming from juries having unequal access to knowledge. Surely informed differences are not as bad as uninformed ones. Two different juries in matching cases could come up with different verdicts for many different reasons, and when such a thing happens the sky does not fall. We expect humans, whether they are judges or juries, to come to different decisions on complex matters. The best thing we can do to promote as much consistency as possible is to ensure juries are equally informed. This means telling jury members about crucial information — such as the power to nullify — that some might know and others not. It is much more worrisome when juries make different decisions because one is more informed than the other.

And surely our goal with juries is not consistency; it is justice. If we eliminate nullification by suppressing it we eliminate one means of finding justice. If Dickson's fear came true and in similar trials one jury nullified, to prevent a legal injustice, and another did not, then surely one case of justice prevailing is better than none.

In addition to those already mentioned, there are many other sources of unfairness and inequality in our courts. Sometimes public opinion will influence the courts; sometimes judges will have personal feelings that affect their actions in court, to the benefit or detriment of defendants. Sometimes prosecutors will, as in Latimer's first trial, feel hostile to the accused and press the maximum charges; others will be sympathetic and press lesser charges.

Our courtrooms are rife with unfairness and unequal treatment. There are things we can do about this, such as increasing legal aid funding. But suppressing jury nullification is not one of them. That only makes the problem worse.

RACISM

Racist juries have given jury nullification a bad name. The case of Emmett Till in particular raises the spectre of white men getting away with lynching in the American South. Certainly that happened, and it was indeed ugly. But jury independence cannot bear the whole blame for this; there was an evident social pathology in the American South that, today, is only partially remedied. Lynching no longer occurs, but there is still a strong undercurrent of racism and extreme conservatism on social issues.

The Till case (see Chapter 2) is often used as the trump card in arguments against the power to nullify. But there were a lot of contributing problems in Mississippi in 1955. There was extreme prejudice exhibited by the prosecutors and other civil authorities, and malfunctioning of the entire justice system. The sheriff's lies, for example, were a key to the verdict. However, no one cites this case as a reason to limit the powers of sheriffs or prosecutors just because they performed very badly in this case.

It was the jury that bore the brunt of criticism for corruption in the justice system in that small town in Mississippi, a corruption that went far deeper than the jury. Sometimes, in fact, juries have defeated such corruption by refusing to convict, as in cases of trials of escaped slaves or of those who aided escaping slaves. But it is not surprising that at times juries too have been swept up in the rampant prejudice prevalent in their social environment.

The problem, however, is not the freedom of juries. How do we suppose the trial of Till's murderers would have gone had the verdict been directed by the bench or otherwise controlled by state authorities? The problem was that a white racist community was, evidently, not going to convict white racist defendants for killing a black man. The problem was pervasive racism.

Till's murderers were set free by a malignant and pervasive social pathology that had spread throughout the white community.

Juries that do indulge in racism or other forms of unacceptable prejudice do so because of prevailing societal bigotry, and they are likely to do so whether or not they are explicitly informed about their power to nullify the law. When jury members share a deep prejudice that destroys their objectivity — for example, believing that a black man who was murdered deserved what he got — they may come to a decision informed by that prejudice.

Highly prejudiced juries are going to find some way of circumventing the intention of the law, whatever is said to them. Therefore, withholding information about the power of juries to nullify only affects normal and likely well-intentioned juries, not highly prejudiced ones. Normal juries, in the absence of information to the contrary, and with judges strongly urging them to follow the law, will not likely nullify the law, whether or not they feel that justice is being served in coming to a verdict of guilty. Prejudiced juries will, by dint of the strength of their feelings, nullify whether or not they are told that they can, seizing if necessary on ridiculous pretexts such as the sheriff's expressed doubt about the identity of the body in Till's case.

Justice Dickson cited the possibility of racism as a reason to ban talk of nullification in the courtroom. He did not, however, cite that as a reason to abolish prosecutors, judges, or the testimony of sheriffs, who might also be racists and contribute to a racially motivated verdict.

Racism can corrupt any sort of human activity and it warps those who indulge in it. It is wrong to single out a particular legal procedure, like jury nullification, and suggest that it has a special link to racism. It is also worth pointing out that even in the horrible Till case, the resulting abuse of the power of jury independence caused such social outrage that Till's name became rallying cry for the American civil rights movement.

On December 1, 1955, in Montgomery, Alabama, Rosa Parks refused the order from a bus driver to give up her seat to a white passenger. Arrested for violating Alabama's segregation laws, Parks became a key symbol of resistance to segregation in the American South. She cited the Till case as a reason for deciding to resist.

Jury independence is a right that can be abused, like any other right. That is insufficient reason to suppress it.

It is also worth questioning the relevance of the racism argument to present-day Canadian life. It is difficult to imagine a twenty-first-century Canadian jury behaving like Till's jury in 1950s Mississippi. If a jury here behaved like that one, nullified the law, and declared a technically guilty defendant to be not guilty, and if the grounds for that decision were indeed questionable, it would cause a uproar of public indignation, as it did in the United States in 1955. A guilty person might go free but the social circumstances that allowed such a thing to happen would come under very close public scrutiny, and it would be unlikely to happen again.

Most aspects of any legal system are subject to abuse. Most principles and doctrines of justice are subject to being used in unjust or harmful ways. The writ of *habeas corpus*, for example, is the right of the imprisoned to petition the court for a hearing to assess the legitimacy of imprisonment. The writ has been described by the US Supreme Court as "one of the centerpieces of our liberties," but as also having:

. . . potentialities for evil as well as for good. Abuse of the writ may undermine the orderly administration of justice and therefore weaken the forces of authority that are essential for civilization.

Similarly, jury independence has the potential for evil as well as good. So does the granting of bail, so does parole, so does a judge giving instructions to a jury, so does the hearing of witnesses. How could any basic principle of justice be otherwise, given the complexity of humans and the imprecise nature of justice?

Our task in the continuing process of building a justice system is not to strike down or suppress important principles because they allow the possibility of abuse, but to attempt to employ them in ways that are fair, non-discriminatory, and in the public interest. Such desirable employment of jury independence will come not from suppression but from open acknowledgement of the idea and public awareness of its importance.

NOT A RIGHT – JUST A POWER

It is accepted belief in legal circles that the ability to nullify is not a "right" of juries but a "power" they have, or, to repeat Justice Dickson's phrase, it is a matter of "de facto discretion" that is less than a right. Justice Dickson argues this in the 1988 Morgentaler judgment, quoted in Chapter 5. Dickson's comment relies heavily on the case *United States vs. Dougherty (1972)*. After finding Dickson's arguments on nullification less than persuasive, I wondered if his source, the author of the Dougherty judgment, would be more so. The major points made about nullification in that judgment are reviewed in the Chapter Notes. If you read only one Chapter Note, read this one!

A similar point about rights and power was made by Justice Fish in the Supreme Court ruling in the Krieger case (see Chapter 2). Fish wrote:

It has . . . been well established that under the system of justice we have inherited from England juries are not entitled as a matter of

*right to refuse to apply the law — but they have the power to do so
when their consciences permit no other course.*

But how can it be said that juries have the power but not the right to
nullify?

This is a critical point in justifying Dickson's prohibition on mentioning nullification in court: if there is a *right* to nullify, then it is hard
to justify not telling jurors about it. He refers in his comments to the
Dougherty case (see Chapter Notes) as establishing the distinction, but
there is no more of a compelling argument there than Dickson's own
declaratory one.

A right is usually thought of as an entitlement, whether it be "natural,"
as in basic human rights — such as life, liberty and the pursuit of happi-
ness — or "civil," which refers to rights we have in relation to the rights
of the state. The right to trial by jury is a widely acknowledged civil right:
it protects us against arbitrary exercise of power by the state.

As established following the Penn trial (see Chapter 3), in order to
accomplish this task, juries must be independent — they must be able
to nullify the law. So how can it make sense to say that we have a right
to a jury trial, on the one hand, but not one with an independent jury,
on the other?

Our *Charter of Rights and Freedoms* enshrines the right to independent juries by specifying the right to the "benefit" of a trial by jury: as
discussed in Chapter 7, "benefit" can have no meaning if juries are not
independent.

Since the accused in Canada have the right to an independent jury,
which is free to exercise jury nullification, it follows that juries have the
right to nullify. It would make no sense to say that, yes, if taken to trial,
we are entitled to have our juries nullify the law, but that juries themselves have no such entitlement.

Claiming juries have this power, but not this entitlement — this right —
comes from a judicial inclination to place nullification on a lower moral

plane than jury trials themselves. Somehow juries can nullify, but it is really not a right: it is to be considered a naked exercise of power, not blessed with the ascription of a right. But juries and jury independence are inseparable. Juries make no sense — they have no value — if not independent, with the ability to nullify. If jury trials are considered a right, then independence and nullification are a necessary part of that right.

Why, we might ask, is this necessary freedom for juries so disparaged that legal commentators are reluctant to call it a right? Why is it considered something less than other freedoms — for example, freedom of speech? Is it because jury freedom has been used at times for bad purposes such as racism? But so has freedom of speech, and that freedom is valued no less because of such abuses. Jury freedom — the right to make independent decisions — is, like other freedoms, a cornerstone of our justice system. Yet it alone is morally downgraded, by some, from a right to a mere power.

Often it is argued that a power is different from a right in that it is something that can be done but is not condoned by society. A judge, for example, has the power to make unfair rulings, but we would not say he has the right to do so. But nullification is not like that. There are good and long-established reasons for allowing jury independence: we have it because, unlike unfair decisions by judges, it is an integral part of our legal system. The one, the judge's unfair decision, is an aberration and an abuse of power that does not deserve to be graced with being called a right. The other is a fully sanctioned entitlement of juries, and as such warrants being called a right.

JURIES MUST BE SELF-MOTIVATED

This argument arises in the ruling made in the Dougherty appeal case cited by Justice Dickson (see Chapter 5). In that case an American appeal court ruled, two to one, that juries should not be told about the possibility of nullification because:

. . . the jury must feel strongly about the values involved in the case,
so strongly that it must itself identify the case as establishing a call
of high conscience, and must independently initiate and undertake
an act in contravention of the established instructions.

This seemingly reasonable point, made in the majority opinion given by judges Leventhal and Adams, actually makes no real sense at all. The idea is that only a powerful upwelling of concern from the jurors themselves, about the justice of applying the law, that would lead a jury to go against the law. Otherwise, I guess, the concern is not genuine or substantive. But what if the concern is deeply felt but the jury does not understand that nullification is a possibility? Juries that might have such an upwelling of conscience are steered away from acting on it by the courts. They are urged at every turn to follow the law and, as in the case of the Latimer jury, are likely to think that they must do so — especially when no one tells them otherwise.

Moreover, well-intentioned juries who want to do the right thing are unlikely to even contemplate going against what the judge says they should do. It is more likely that only dysfunctional ones, like those for the trials of the Donnelly or of Emmett Till murderers (see Chapter 2), will act perversely and refuse to convict, whatever they are told or not told.

Insisting that nullification is legitimate only when it spontaneously erupts from an uninformed jury is imposing an arbitrary and unreasonable restriction on this fundamental right of juries.

The Dougherty ruling that uses this dubious argument also contains devastating dissent comments from Judge Bazelon, who was outvoted by two junior and less distinguished judges on the appeal panel (see Chapter Notes for more on this). Bazelon describes the argument used by the two other judges as being that:

. . . the spontaneous and unsolicited act of nullification is thought
less likely, on the whole, to reflect bias and a perverse sense of val-

THE ARGUMENTS AGAINST JURY INDEPENDENCE

ues than the act of nullification carried out by a jury carefully instructed on its power and responsibility.

But, he goes on to write:

It seems substantially more plausible to me to assume that the very opposite is true. The juror motivated by prejudice seems to me more likely to make spontaneous use of the power to nullify, and more likely to disregard the judge's exposition of the normally controlling legal standards.

Bazelon continues to shred the majority opinion in this appeal ruling by pointing out further inconsistencies in that opinion. Apparently, according to Leventhal and Adams, it is bad for juries *to know* they can nullify. Logically this would suggest that jurors who know about nullification should be excluded from juries, but Leventhal and Adams contradict their point by stating that "informal communication" to the jury (by which they mean prior knowledge gained from the media and other sources) "generally conveys adequately the idea of [nullification.]" So is it good thing for juries to spontaneously and in ignorance come to the idea of nullifying the law, as Leventhal and Adams argue, or is it good, as they also argue, that juries know of the idea already, without the need to be told? Leventhal and Adams seem to have no difficulty in contradicting themselves.

As I mention in the Chapter Notes on this case, it is surprising and distressing to note that Justice Dickson relied so heavily on the arguments of Leventhal and Adams, arguments that are almost comically contradictory and specious. It is all the more troubling when Leventhal and Adams are so thoroughly and effectively refuted in the same document, in the dissent written by the highly distinguished Judge Bazelon.

Justice Dickson justified his far-reaching ban on mentioning nullification in the courtroom by quoting the words of Leventhal and Adams,

THE SECRET POWER OF JURIES

ignoring the far more insightful and intelligent words of Bazelon. Why did he do this? One can only assume that his antipathy toward nullification blinded him to looking at the real arguments in favour of it, seeking instead to quote an argument, no matter how fatuous, supporting what appears to have been his own personal bias.

INTERFERING WITH JUDICIAL AUTHORITY

Judges in Canada represent high accomplishment in a very competitive field. There are many very skilled lawyers, and some of the best of them are chosen to be judges.

Judges pride themselves on being experts in the law — that has been the focus of their careers. They rightly see the law as the backbone of society: the law keeps things straight and ensures that reason and order prevail. They see the law as the most essential part of the preservation of our rights and freedoms; without the law there would be no universal rights or freedoms.

It is a praiseworthy aspect of our justice system that trials have judges who can use their understanding of the law to instruct juries from the perspective of one with deep knowledge of the law.

Juries consist of more or less randomly selected citizens with no special access to legal information, and they rely heavily, therefore, on what judges tell them about the law. Judges usually point out that they, as experts, will tell juries what the law is, and then tell them that the job of the jury is to determine the facts in a case (did the defendant actually do what he or she is accused of doing?). There is a strong implication here that juries should not worry themselves about whether or not they agree with the law; they should just decide on guilt or innocence according to the law.

A judge has control over much of what goes on in the courtroom and can make all sorts of rulings, such as on the admissibility of evidence, the conduct of jury members, and the nature of the questions asked of witnesses. Judges can even dismiss a case if they believe the evidence is too weak to convict. They have a lot of power in a trial.

But, in theory at least, and as much as they might try to convince the jury otherwise, they do not have control over the single most significant element in a jury trial: the verdict.

It is human nature to resent that which one cannot control, and all the more so when one controls everything else except that one thing. It is easier for a person with limited control over a situation to accept those parts he or she does not control, than for a person who controls almost everything to accept the one part that is out of his or her hands. This is especially true when that one thing is the biggest thing, like the verdict in a criminal trial.

That, in part at least, is why judges are so leery of jury nullification: in their eyes their control has been usurped, and not by another qualified person, but by amateurs.

One can understand the psychology of why judges resent their loss of control, and one can see why it would be particularly galling to lose out to amateurs. But the law, that to which they are so dedicated, is sometimes an ass (as Mr. Bumble pointed out in *Oliver Twist*), and it falls to ordinary citizens on a jury to point that out when necessary.

It is right that judges dedicate themselves to supporting the law; it would be a conflict in roles if they had to declare a law to be unjust. But they ought not to unduly suppress juries' ability to point out when the law is an ass.

THE JUROR'S OATH

Opponents of jury nullification often claim that when jurors take the oath at the beginning of a trial they are swearing to make a decision that is in accord with the law. Is that correct?

The *Criminal Code of Canada* simply says that an oath will be sworn, but the exact form of the oath is not specified. The general approach taken to oaths in Canada is illustrated on the Justice BC website:

> *By taking the juror's oath, you are making a legal commitment to participate in making a fair decision on the guilt or innocence of the defendant.*

This guideline suggests nothing about following the law; in fact, by stressing fairness it would seem to invite the possibility of nullification. The actual wording of oaths in particular jurisdictions, however, is usually more ambiguous: typically the oaths entail a commitment to carry out the jury member's tasks faithfully and impartially, and "to render a true verdict according to the evidence."

It is the latter statement — agreeing to a true verdict according to the evidence — that is often taken to mean that jurors are bound to base their decision on only the facts of what happened and relate that to the law. They can, for example, determine that Morgentaler broke the law by carrying out abortions in violation of the law. But they cannot, according to this view of the oath, say that applying the law would be unjust. That would be going beyond the evidence, supposedly violating the oath.

But that view of the oath makes unwarranted assumptions about what it means. What is a true verdict according to the evidence? Is it the verdict that comes from strictly following the letter of the law? Is it a true verdict if it represents, in a juror's mind, false justice? Is not a true verdict one that a juror thinks reflects true justice, regardless of the law?

And what, we may ask, does "evidence" mean? Evidence is not necessarily just what is presented in court, but can also be reasonable conclusions one draws from that evidence. It is evidence when the facts in a case reveal the injustice of a particular law, or of the application of a law in a particular case.

There was evidence that Robert Latimer killed his daughter, but there was also evidence that it was an act of love and mercy, and therefore evidence that it was different from most murders. When Rosa Parks defied the bus driver's order in 1955 she violated Alabama's segregation laws. But who, aside from racists, would countenance a conviction based upon violating such laws? The racist nature of such laws is an issue of real relevance to a jury; it is part of the evidence in the case.

If the oath was intended to limit jurors only to the direct evidence brought up in court — facts — and not to make any inferences from that evidence, then that oath would have to make some such explicit statement. But how then could the jury sensibly function? If one could not make inferences, how could anything be proven? A man shoots in the direction of another man, who is hit by a bullet and dies. We make the inference that the first man shot the second man and killed him.

If the oath were intended to enforce strict compliance with the law, there would be much clearer ways of putting it, such as:

I swear to come to a verdict that is consistent with the law.

Or, even more explicitly:

I swear that my verdict will reflect only the law and not my conscience, should the two differ.

But either of those would violate the principle of jury independence and would not be acceptable for the reasons cited in the previous chapter. Even most judges acknowledge that juries cannot be prevented from nullifying, so the oath could not so specify. Instead the oath is devised in convoluted legal language that makes it sound like jurors are bound to follow the law, but does not actually say or mean that.

Most jurors in fact probably have no idea what they are swearing to, thinking the oath is simply a formal commitment to proceed in an honest way, like the oaths sworn by witnesses to tell the truth. It will not likely occur to many of them that the oath is designed to lead them away from exercising their power to nullify.

* * *

Lysander Spooner in his great *Essay on Trial by Jury*, published in 1852, quoted Blackstone's rendition of the oath from a hundred years earlier, a form that is similar to oaths used in England, Canada, and the USA today:

> *Well and truly to try, and true deliverance make, between our sovereign lord, the king, and the prisoner whom they have in charge, and a true verdict to give according to the evidence.*

Spooner, too, challenged the notion that the phrase "a true verdict according to the evidence" required jurors to come to a verdict just derived from the facts of the case and to leave the legalities — what constitutes grounds for a judgment of guilt or innocence — to the court.

Spooner essentially says that no oath can override the truth of a situation. "Guilt," he wrote, "is an intrinsic quality of actions, and can neither be created, destroyed nor changed by legislation." He goes on to write:

> *No [court] that attempts to try this issue can have any moral right to declare a man guilty, for an act that is intrinsically innocent, at the bidding of a legislature, any more than at the bidding of anyone else. And this oath does not require or permit a jury to do so.*

Spooner continues by saying that the words "according to the evidence," if taken to mean "such evidence only as the government sees fit to allow to go to the jury," would be a violation of both common law and Magna Carta. In other words, "according to the evidence" must be taken to mean whatever the jury considers relevant, not just what the law or the court claims is relevant evidence.

PLACING UNDUE STRAIN UPON THE JURY

I mention this only because it is sometimes used as a justification for suppressing jury independence, not because it has any real merit.

The argument goes along these lines (although usually in less stark language): jury members are a bunch of amateurs anyway and are already over their heads in trying to understand the law as it is. How can we expect them to take on the onerous task of deciding to override the law? This, it is argued, would be unfair to them.

But what about the strain, and the possible lifetime of regret, one could have for voting against one's own conscience? How distressed must Latimer's jurors be whenever they think of the unnecessary, uncalled-for grief their decision has brought upon this man and his family?

Defending Ted and Rose Bates (see Chapter 2) lawyer Harry Ludgate warned the jurors that the wrong decision (guilt) could give them "sleepless nights when it was too late to correct a mistake." Ludgate knew that a guilty verdict for this hapless pair, and sending them to the gallows, would haunt jurors afterwards.

There can be few more stressful acts than to deliberately act against one's conscience and cause harm to a fellow human. Those who have genuine concern about strain on jury members might better argue that juries be told that they are not constrained to verdicts as directed by the law, and that in circumstances where their consciences demand they go against such a verdict, they are free to do so.

CAUSING AN EPIDEMIC OF NULLIFICATIONS

Would, as some fear, open acknowledgment of a jury's power to nullify result in widespread and profligate use of the power? This seems highly unlikely. The Chicago Jury Project of the 1950s examined many issues related to juries and found that jury nullification will be used only infrequently for four reasons (the Jury Project statements are in italics):

1) *The law has adjusted to prevailing values.* Nullification is likely to arise only when jury members find the law to be at odds with community standards and values, and these cases are rare. In a democracy the law is an expression of the will of the community and it continually evolves to meet community interests.

2) *The group nature of the jury curbs eccentric views.* Justice Dickson in his Supreme Court of Canada ruling in the Morgentaler judgment worried about someone "being acquitted by a jury who, with reformist zeal, wanted to express disapproval of the . . . law." But a jury generally consists of twelve people, so all twelve would have to share in this "reformist zeal." It seems more likely that the integrity of the court would be threatened when just one eccentric or zealous individual can influence the proceedings, such as a judge or a prosecutor.

3) *The jury is solemnly invested with an important public task.* Judges take great pains to explain the law, the importance of the law, and the obligation of juries to respect the law. It is only in extreme situations that juries are likely to want to override these injunctions.

4) *The jury is never told that it has the power to nullify.* Because the judge does not tell the jury about its power to nullify, most juries will not even be aware that they have such power. This, I should add, is not in my view an acceptable situation, as argued throughout this

book; this silence is a violation of the *Charter*, civil liberties, and common sense. How can it be wrong to tell a jury what it has the power to do? But even if juries could be so informed, say by the defence lawyer, nullification would still be a rarity because of the other reasons given in the Chicago Jury Project.

There is another reason why nullification would not often occur even if a defence lawyer could mention it. In pleading for nullification a lawyer would be using a last resort, because such a defence entails the tacit admission that the defendant might be technically guilty. That is a risk lawyers would generally prefer to avoid; most juries will take their obligation to the law seriously and would be inclined to nullify in only extreme circumstances. Appealing for nullification in a profligate manner could well irritate juries and turn them against a defendant, or even make them question evidence they had previously considered to be exculpatory. Appealing for nullification would be a risky choice in most cases.

UPSETTING THE BALANCE

Dickson's final argument, quoting the Dougherty appeal judgment, was that:

> *An equilibrium has evolved — an often marvelous balance — with the jury acting as a "safety valve" for exceptional cases . . .*

There had been some sort of reasonable equilibrium before Dickson made his statement on the matter in the Morgentaler ruling. There had been a balance such that the conviction of Morgentaler, which would not have been in accord with community standards of justice, was not possible. Is it balanced after Dickson's statement? Ask Latimer.

CHAPTER 9

WHAT CAN JURORS DO? WHAT CAN YOU DO?

THE VULNERABILITY OF THE JURY SYSTEM

Jury independence, a cornerstone of the jury system, is under siege in Canada and elsewhere. What is at stake is nothing less than the continuing viability of juries. For what purpose is there in retaining a cumbersome and expensive courtroom procedure if it must simply reflect the views of the presiding judge?

Already the device of summary convictions — proceeding against a defendant without indictment or trial — is increasingly being used in Canada to speed up proceedings, save money, and relieve pressure on courtrooms.

One often reads commentaries suggesting that juries no longer have much purpose. While writing this conclusion in the early spring of 2013, I happened across an article by English lawyer Harry Mount in the *London Telegraph* headlined "Have juries had their day in court?" He cites an old concern — jury members' lack of understanding of complex issues — and a new one: through the Internet and social media, jurors now have access to knowledge about witnesses and defendants that they ought not to have. Mount talked of a former chief justice who wanted judges to be allowed into jury rooms so they "could know how to direct them better." Mount stops short of arguing for the elimination of juries, ending with:

We still prefer to put our lives in the hands of 12 men and women, however angry and misguided they might be.

That is not exactly a ringing endorsement of juries, especially from someone who claims to support them. With friends like this, can the jury system be expected to survive in Britain?

And don't say it could not happen here. As it is, in Canada jury trials are available only for crimes punishable by at least five years in prison. Hong Kong, with a justice system similarly derived from the British system, does not allow jury trials in district courts, which have the right to impose sentences of up to seven years. India did away with juries altogether in 1960, mostly on the basis of single case (see Nanavati, Chapter 2). Singapore and South Africa abolished juries in 1969.

There is more at stake here than a few instances when a jury might save a defendant from the unjust application of a law. What is at stake is not just jury independence, but whether or not we are going to have juries at all.

Many commentators have noted juries without the power to go against the law would be of little value. Such power represents the only real advantage they have over judges - it is the only real "benefit" they can bring to a defendant. (See Constitutional argument, Chapter 7.) Judges are pretty much obliged to follow the letter of the law; juries are not. But if the role of juries is narrowed is simply to evaluate and adjudicate evidence, and to determine compliance with law, then there are much better ways we accomplish that task, such as a panel of judges. Judges have extensive training and experience in understanding the law and evaluating evidence. Juries consist of laypersons without detailed knowledge of the law and probably without much experience in evaluating complex sources of evidence. If strict compliance with law is what we want, then in almost every conceivable way judges would be better then juries. Juries blocked from making extralegal considerations would essentially be expensive and cumbersome ceremonial entities. And they would then likely come to be seen as irrelevant and disposable impediments to efficient courtroom procedures. Suppressing jury nullification, then, strikes at the heart of meaningful jury system.

BREAKTHROUGH IN NEW HAMPSHIRE

While at present the tradition of jury trials continues in most justice systems derived from English law, this issue remains unclear and mostly unresolved, even hundreds of years after the trial of William Penn decisively established the need for jury independence. Supporters and opponents of jury independence continue to be in conflict in Canada, Britain, the United States, Australia, New Zealand, and probably elsewhere.

In the United States, with juries under the control of state legislatures, there are many different approaches to the issue of jury independence. Most of them are not friendly to the idea. A recent essay in an American magazine for legal professionals (*The Champion*) discussed how the idea of nullification was once widely accepted in American courts but now "has become the unspoken secret of the American jury deliberation room. No longer may juries freely disregard laws that they believe to be unjust."

In New Hampshire, however, there was a remarkable recent breakthrough. On June 18, 2012, Governor John Lynch signed *House Bill 146*, which reads:

> *In all criminal proceedings the court shall permit the defense to inform the jury of its right to judge the facts and the application of the law in relation to the facts in controversy.*

Finally, after 340 years, here it is! A jurisdiction had the courage and honesty to settle the matter openly. Defence lawyers can inform juries in New Hampshire of their right to nullify the law. Hallelujah!

On the other hand, this right to fully inform juries has been strongly discouraged in other American states, as it has been in Canada. In most states, defence lawyers are forbidden from mentioning nullification. In California the jury oath comes very close to forbidding nullification, and during the selection process prospective jurors can be asked about their views on nullification and excluded if they show any support for the idea. Jurors who do not admit to having such views, but who then advocate nullification in jury deliberations, can later be prosecuted for perjury. Even worse, California jurors are required to inform on other jurors if one of them argues that the law should not be followed.

Consider the difference in how the same case would be handled in New Hampshire and, say, California. Juries, if they know they can do so, are generally reluctant to convict for minor drug charges. A majority of Americans think their anti-drug laws are far too punitive. In New Hampshire, on September 19, 2012, soon after the state passed its jury nullification law, Doug Darrell was found not guilty for growing a small number of marijuana plants in his back yard.

Darrell was fifty-nine years old and had four grown children. A piano tuner and woodworker, he had been married for nearly forty years. His marijuana plants, grown for his personal use, were discovered when spotted by a National Guard helicopter. Charged with cultivation, he faced up to seven years in prison. Commonly in such cases there is a plea bargain, giving a lesser sentence in return for a guilty plea. But Darrell refused this and, then, probably thanks to the new law, was not convicted and was set free.

This is a classic case of a victimless crime, the penalties for which far exceed community standards for such offences. In New Hampshire the result was a verdict of not guilty. In California, had Darrell refused to plea bargain, he might well have been given the full seven years. And for what purpose?

Plea bargaining, by the way, has become a nasty tool in prosecutions for minor drug offenses, particularly in the United States. Typically a very severe charge will be brought against a drug offender, allowing the prosecutor to achieve an easy conviction by then reaching a comprom-ise. Under federal law in the United States, growing fifty or more mari-juana plants can lead to a prison sentence of twenty years. Five years in prison is a common compromise for such offences. Fearing the longer sentence, most defendants will make a deal for, say, five years, giving up their right to a jury trial. Now, in New Hampshire at least, many more may be willing to take a chance that their fellow citizens will refuse to find them guilty. With nullification in the offing, the ridiculously severe penalties will actually work in favour of the accused. Who would want to send Darrell to prison for seven years, or someone with a few more plants to prison for twenty years?

The public's distaste for convicting those guilty of these victim-less crimes parallels the situation in the Prohibition Era, when people charged with consuming alcohol were routinely found not guilty. Nulli-fications for minor drug offences may happen much more often now, in New Hampshire, although given that strong possibility, prosecutors may be less inclined to prosecute. Either case — more nullifications or fewer prosecutions — will surely result in a more sane approach to minor drug offences in New Hampshire.

WHAT CAN WE DO ABOUT IT?

What can we do in Canada, where nullification is so strongly suppressed by the Supreme Court? There are at least four ways the matter could be resolved in a positive manner:

1) Legislation, like the legislation in New Hampshire, could be passed allowing defence lawyers to make a plea for nullification.

WHAT CAN JURORS DO? WHAT CAN YOU DO?

Opposition is likely to be strong against any such movement, even if some politician or, better, some political party were to take up the cause. In the United States an organization called the Fully Informed Jury Association (FIJA) has been promoting awareness of jury nullification to both potential jurors and politicians. They provide examples of nullification-friendly legislation similar to that passed in New Hampshire. They have handed out pamphlets on courtroom steps to potential jurors, much as Julian Heicklen did (see Chapter 1), and go even further by trying to notify jurors in particular cases (Heicklen was just handing out pamphlets at random). Such targeted lobbying has been deemed illegal, but the perpetrators rarely get arrested. Authorities probably fear that bringing charges against them would necessitate producing the pamphlets in court, thereby informing their jury about their right to nullify.

Although I strongly support FIJA in regard to jury independence, I am a little leery of that organization's connection with the American libertarian movement. Libertarians promote freedom from any sort of authority, and freeing juries is a natural focus of interest for them. Many of them support other good causes, such as a woman's right to choose, and opposition to international military adventurism. But some others, in my view, go much too far in their opposition to government and their endorsement of Ayn Rand's notion of the virtue of selfishness.

I support nullification not because it is an attack on government oppression, but because it is a way to seek justice and curb the inflexibility of certain laws in certain situations. My concern about FIJA is guilt by association: if it becomes the face of the jury independence movement then its broader libertarian beliefs might turn away many potential supporters. The argument for jury independence and nullification stands on its own — entirely separate from the ideas of libertarianism — as a means of creating greater fairness in our justice system.

2) The Supreme Court of Canada could rescind its ruling which prevents defence lawyers from making a plea for nullification.

Recognizing that Justice Dickson went too far in his suppression of jury nullification would be a simple way to resolve the untenable situation in Canada. As discussed earlier, his ruling not only violates the *Charter of Rights and Freedoms* in a couple ways (it is discriminatory and it removes the prescribed "benefit" of jury trials), it also violates the basic civil liberty of entitlement to the best possible defence.

We should not, however, hold our breaths on this one.

3) A lawyer could challenge the constitutionality of the Supreme Court's ruling by making a plea for nullification.

I have wondered what would happen if a lawyer tried this — if, for example, Latimer's lawyer had tried a nullification defence in defiance of the Supreme Court's ruling. Such a strategy would probably go nowhere as it would immediately be ruled out of order, and any lawyer who persisted might face a mistrial and possible punishment. There is perhaps one sliver of a chance of such a plea being made, based upon the nature of Justice Dickson's original statement, which might not be fully binding because it was *obiter dictum*, a side issue attached only loosely to the main judgment in the Morgentaler ruling. This is a complex legal matter and is discussed at greater length in Chapter Notes. As explained there, the prospects for a legal challenge are not great.

But it would be very interesting if a *Charter* appeal could somehow be launched — a Charter appeal against the Supreme Court's own ruling. The Supreme Court, too, is obliged to honour the *Charter*. That in fact is its job.

WHAT CAN YOU DO?

There is no sign that any of the remedies to the current suppression of jury nullification will soon take place in Canada. One can only hope that growing public awareness will result, at some point, in something happening to reverse the prevailing Supreme Court nullification of nullification. We should do everything possible to inform potential jury members of their rights.

Since you have read this book you will now be informed. You can tell others about the issues raised here. Maybe through modern means of communication, such as social media, word can spread. If the possibility of nullification becomes widely known and understood then it will not matter so much if defence lawyers can tell juries about it — some juries will know anyway.

Informed citizens who are called to jury duty can bring their knowledge of the possibility of nullification to the deliberations of juries. One must be careful about this, however, because it might well be the case that others on the jury are not so informed. In order to be effective, your knowledge needs to be handled in a circumspect way.

The first consideration is to make sure that one really wants to invoke nullification in a particular case. It would be irresponsible to advocate nullification in any situation other than one where it seems clear that following the law would bring about what a juror believes to be a genuine injustice. We do live in a democracy and ought not to casually support going against the apparent will of the elected majority, unless the circumstances in a particular trial truly demand doing so. We would not want to live in a society where the rule of law is not respected and where juries showed such disrespect in a profligate manner.

We should advocate nullifying a law only when we strongly believe that justice is being thwarted by adherence to the law. How do we know when this is the case? It is a matter of judgment, and because it is a difficult question, with many factors to consider — the importance of rule of law, the presumptiveness of assuming we know better than the law, the danger of turning public sympathy away from jury independence, and others — we should be very cautious about it. But when it is very clear, when our consciences tell us that, as a matter of simple human decency, as a matter of mercy and compassion, as a matter of evident fairness, the law is coming up short, one must step in and try to intervene.

Recall Henry Morgentaler's story about why he had to help people in trouble, how he was driven by:

> . . . the image of someone drowning on a river or lake, and all you had to do was to stretch out your arm to save them. Would you do it if there was a sign saying "it is forbidden to help"? I knew I could not obey that sign. I would obey a higher morality.

Similarly, if a juror sees someone drowning in the bureaucratic inflexibility of a law, he or she should then reach out to save that person.

When should a jury member consider nullification? The following circumstances are examples of when one might do so:

1) The law in question is too repressive, as in the Penn, Zenger, and Morgentaler cases. The law in these cases was not in accord with public sentiment, and the juries' refusal to find guilt was, in effect, a protest against the law. Modern equivalents of this are prosecutions for minor marijuana offences: there is little public sympathy for these because the laws in Canada and particularly in the United States are generally seen as far too severe. There are many drug cases where this concern arises and an increasing number where

juries simply refuse to convict. Examples include the Krieger case in Canada and the Darrell case in New Hampshire. Another case in Montana was recently thrown out because impartial jurors — ones who might be willing to convict — could not be found.

2) The law is not sufficiently discriminating, as in the Latimer case. Although it has often been recommended, Canada has no law regarding "compassionate homicide." As it is, we have only the very blunt legal instrument of a murder charge for the deliberate ending of a life. Some compassionate prosecutors find ways around a murder charge by creative indictments (as discussed earlier), but some do not. The charge of murder against Latimer led to a penalty that, in the eyes of his judge and jury, was far too severe. They recognized that his action was a compassionate one and wanted only a token sentence.

3) Protest against official misconduct, as in the Pritchard and Oldrich case. The British government's support for the invasion of Iraq was the source of great controversy and juries were reluctant to convict protestors, so long as they did not do too much damage. Many people would find it difficult to convict if they viewed the protestors' actions as being in opposition to immoral actions on the part of their own government.

4) There is no point in enforcing a law, as in the cases of Bateses and Latimer. Who would have wanted to see Tim and Rose Bates hang? And who, other than those with strong and entrenched views about end-of-life issues, would have wanted Robert Latimer to serve ten years in prison? He, like the Bateses, was no threat to offend again, and like them he had already suffered the agony of watching his child die. Why make these unfortunate people suffer again?

There are probably other circumstances in which one might want to argue for nullifying the law. But having read this book, how should one handle possible jury duty?

First, regarding getting on a jury, there should be no particular problem in Canada; it is largely a matter of chance. All that is normally given to the prosecutor and the defence lawyer is your name and occupation. They can see you, so they will know if you are a man or woman and if you are a member of a visually identifiable group or have some other distinguishing physical feature. Such superficial characteristics should not, of course, affect whether or not you are selected, but that is entirely up to the lawyers. They need not explain their decisions. On rare occasions one side or the other can challenge the composition of a jury if, for example, it does not seem sufficiently balanced in terms of race or gender.

In the Canadian selection procedure, unlike in the American one, questions are usually very limited. Morris Manning was able to push against this restriction a bit in his defence of Morgentaler (see Chapter 4) by being allowed to ask prospective jurors about their beliefs about abortion, but this was unusual. Prospective American jurors, on the other hand, can be intensively quizzed on anything related to possible bias in the case, while in Canada it is generally assumed that jurors will follow judicial instructions to be unbiased.

So we in Canada do not have the problem that exists in some states, such as California, where anyone having sympathy with the possibility of nullifying would have trouble getting past the screening, particularly in trials where nullification might be in play. The prosecutor in California can ask you how you feel about nullification and exclude you if there is a chance your feelings might get in the way of a conviction. And you had better answer the question truthfully or you might be subsequently prosecuted for perjury.

In Canada both the prosecution and defence have a set number of "pre-emptory challenges," which means they can exclude potential jurors for any reason at all. A first-degree murder trial, for example, allows twenty such challenges. However, unless you are carrying a copy of this book, in full view, or wearing a T-shirt proclaiming your support for nullification, there is little chance either side could know your interest in the matter.

It is quite possible, then, that a Canadian jury could have members who are informed about the possibility of nullification. How should one handle this knowledge? First, as mentioned earlier, one must be very cautious about invoking the idea at all. Next, my advice would be not to launch into the matter too soon or too forcefully. It will seem like a strange concept to some of your fellow jurors. See how the discussion is progressing, and if someone says something like "It's too bad our verdict will result in prison sentence," then would be a good time to say, "Well, of course, we do not really have to find the defendant guilty." This will probably open up the discussion on the topic, where more information can be brought out. It is better for the others to be brought along gently, putting pieces together themselves, and gradually becoming more familiar with the idea.

For defence lawyers in cases where nullification is the only real defence, all they can do is to offer some sort of pretext for a verdict of not guilty, and hope that jurors will use that pretext to justify such a verdict. It is slightly absurd that, centuries after the William Penn trial, lawyers have to resort to such tactics and that an open and honest appeal for nullification cannot be made. Lawyers ought to be able to make the simple appeal that was made by Morris Manning in Henry Morgentaler's last trial (also quoted earlier):

> The judge will tell you what the law is. He will tell you about the ingredients of the offence, what the Crown has to prove, what the defenses may be or may not be, and you must take the law from him. But I submit to you that it is up to you and you alone to apply the law to this evidence and you have a right to say it shouldn't be applied.

You have an absolute right, if you become a jury member, to say that a particular law in a particular circumstance should not be applied. And you, having read this book, might be the only person on your jury who knows this.

* * *

I was moved to write this book by my concern at the way our legal system treated Robert Latimer. After reading the transcript of his trial, watching a recording of his Supreme Court hearing, and conducting other research on his story, I became increasingly disturbed by what I was learning. The law simply could not respond to the unfortunate circumstances of this man. In spite of sympathy from most sides, a ten-year imprisonment with a lifetime on parole became inevitable. Even the Supreme Court was sympathetic. While it could not overturn the conviction or his sentence, because both were consistent with the law, the Court pointed out that this was a man who was no danger to society and no threat to re-offend. The Court even took the unusual step of suggesting that Latimer would have a good case for clemency.

I talked to Latimer extensively in 2005 and 2006 while he was in prison and then on day parole from 2007 to 2010. I attended his parole hearing in December 2006 and was stunned by the callous disrespect shown to Latimer by that board, a disrespect that typically falls on those who are convicted of serious crimes. Maybe, I thought at the time, it is all right to treat real murderers this way (although even then I would find it bothersome), but a man whose judge and jury thought a token short sentence would be appropriate, a man described by all who knew him as a good man, a man convicted of a crime that even his prosecutor suggested was an act of love? Was this a way to treat such a man or, really, any man?

The parole board not only treated Latimer with appalling disrespect, it turned down his application for day parole after seven years in prison — seven times longer than his judge and jury had recommended. I wrote a detailed account of the hearing and alerted a friend in the BC Civil Liberties Association as to what had taken place. He talked to lawyer Jason Gratl, also associated with the BCCLA. Gratl took up the case at his own expense and wrote a brilliant appeal brief that carried the day. Latimer got his day parole, only a few months late.

Even then, while on day parole, Latimer was subjected to petty harassment by the parole board. Why? Certainly not because he was a danger to anyone. I guess it was because he was a convicted felon, and that is how the parole board tends to treat such people.

What happened to Latimer was wrong and, after the charges were laid, the only point at which his terrible fate could have been avoided was when the jury came down with its verdict. That was when Latimer could have been set free, and the entire absurd sequence of punitive events that followed could have been stopped. But even though the consequences of their guilty verdict must have given some of the jury members sleepless nights, it was not their fault. It was the fault of judicial aversion to jury nullification and the suppression of the knowledge that likely would have led to a verdict of not guilty. Simply put, the jury was not fully informed.

When we see someone drowning it is not a sense of heroism that motivates us to try to save that person. It is a deeply held feeling that we are our brother's keeper — that we are part of a human community in which we live and survive because we look out for one another. We feel others' pain; we share their grief; we lament their loneliness; we understand that we are all in this life together. We are offended by injustice, maybe doubly so when that injustice is legally sanctioned.

When we have the chance to save a drowning person we should take it for their sake, and for our own.

* * *

In my research for the stories in the first part of this book I was read-ing about slavery in the American South before the abolition of slavery (Amendment XIII, 1865). I was struck by the fact that the American Constitution, prior to the Thirteenth Amendment, actually condoned slavery and protected slave owners. Article IV Section 2 still contains the original (and now superseded) wording:

> *No person held to service or labor in one State, under the laws thereof, escaping into another, shall, in consequence of any law or regulation therein, be discharged from such service or labor; but shall be delivered up on claim of the party, to whom the such ser-vice or labor may be due.*

In other words, slaves are property, no less so when they escape to a state without slavery. They can be claimed back. This clause provided the grounds for the infamous fugitive slave acts of 1793 and 1850 whereby slaves, even those who had escaped to the North, could be tracked down and returned to their "rightful" owners in the South.

The American founding fathers, so revered in American mythology, supported slavery, and their vaunted Constitution legalized and pro-tected it. If there ever was a law that should not have been respected, this was it. And many Americans did refuse to respect it, both by helping escaped slaves and refusing — in defiance of the law — to convict those who did help them.

* * *

Law is necessary for a civilized society, but it is not sacrosanct. It should be respected, but not mindlessly obeyed. The American Constitution, containing a clause condoning the shameful practice of human slavery, showed that even highly respected legal documents must, at times, be opposed. The Nuremburg trials for Nazi war criminals following the

Second World War established for all time (we would hope) that rules and laws must not override our need to protect the dignity and well-being of all people.

We have very few ways of standing up to problematic laws. Let us at least properly inform and empower the ordinary citizens who sit on our juries, so they can intervene with a call for mercy whenever the law fails to serve the demands of justice and human decency.

ACKNOWLEDGEMENTS

Very much of the credit for this work goes to Gwyneth Evans, who tirelessly read and re-read the manuscripts, fixed the language, removed bad ideas, added good ones, carried out research, and provided continuing support and inspiration for this project. Many thanks as well to others who provided help with the manuscript: Mark Battersby, Jean Irwin, Shirley Johnson, and Lea Tassie. Lawyers Alison Campbell, Diana Davison, and Gordon Macdonald gave me much assistance in understanding the law; any dubious legal assertions that may have survived their estimable advice are entirely mine. Morris Manning, the prominent Ontario lawyer who defended Henry Morgentaler, was kind enough to review and add comments to the portion of the book dealing with that trial. Thanks to Peter Gordon, Peter Hicken, and Bob Johnson for providing helpful references.

I deeply appreciate the on-going support and inspiration Bob Rowan has provided for my work. I am grateful as well to James Lorimer, Publisher, who had faith in this project and Cy Strom, Acquisitions Editor, James Lorimer and Co., who has been most helpful in getting this book together, and who repeatedly made excellent and insightful suggestions that much improved it. Thanks as well to Jade Colbert, Kendra Martin, and Nicole Habib for their help in editing the manuscript.

CHAPTER NOTES

PREFACE

THE RULE OF LAW:

Tom Bingham, *The Rule of Law* (London: Allen Lane, 2010).

JURY TRIALS:

Patrick Devlin, *Trial by Jury* (London: Stevens and Sons, 1956).

UNEQUAL JUSTICE IN THE US:

J. Reiman and P. Leighton, *The Rich Get Richer and the Poor Get Prison*, 9th ed. (Boston: Pearson, 2004).

SCALIA QUOTE:

The quote attributed to American Supreme Court Justice Scalia is referred to on many websites, but its origins are murky. Some claim that he never said it and no one to my knowledge has found a source for it. Some claim that it was made in Scalia's dissenting opinion in the Supreme Court's judgment in the case of *Herrera v. Collins 506 US 390 1993*, but it is not there. Others claim that it comes from a speech he gave shortly after the Herrera trial. But they have not produced it.

Why then use the quote at all? Fair question. I used it in part because it is a pithy expression of views that Scalia does appear to hold, and these views are an extreme example of a general judicial predilection for law trumping justice — the central concern of this book. And it is not as though the quoted statement is at odds with Scalia's views. In spite of all the online discussion of the quote, Scalia has, as far as I can determine, never denied making the statement. In fact he has made less quotable but very similar statements in both the Herrera case and the Troy Anthony Davis case (2009, U.S. Lexus 5037, 7 2009):

This Court has never held that the Constitution forbids the execution of a convicted defendant who has had a full and fair trial but is later able to convince a habeas court that he is "actually" innocent.

This has been taken in different ways by different commentators. Some take it simply as a statement of a legal truism, others that it confirms the picture we have of Scalia from the unverified quote: that he would not be too bothered by an innocent person being executed so long as the trial had been "fair." What other evidence can we find that Scalia might be more concerned about legal procedure than even an unjust execution? His views on capital punishment are instructive.

Scalia may not be too worried about an innocent person being executed because he thinks that there has never been an actual case of such a thing in the American justice system, and that the risk of it happening is "insignificant" (see *Justice Denied,* Issue 32, Spring 2006). He made this claim in his opinion in *Kansas v. Marsh, No. 04-1170 2006,* in which he disagreed strongly with the comments of Justice Souter, who pointed out that "hundreds of . . . wrongful convictions in potentially capital cases have been documented over the last century."

Scalia does not think that a death sentence is such a terrible thing anyway. In a widely published 2007 article, "God's Justice and Ours," Scalia wrote that "for the believing Christian death is no big deal," because death is merely going to a better place.

FOR THE " DAMN SYSTEM . . ." QUOTE AND INFORMATION ABOUT THE WEST MEMPHIS THREE AND BENJAMIN SPENCER :

Nathaniel Rich, "The Nightmare of the West Memphis Three," *New York Review of Books,* April 4, 2013.

The West Memphis Three are three men who were convicted as teenagers in 1994 of the murder of three young boys in West Memphis, Arkansas. The evidence was flimsy but it was a time of hysteria about imagined satanic cults, and one of the three was bullied into making a false confession. All three were found guilty and one of them was sentenced to die. Partly on the basis of new evidence they were released in 2011.

CHAPTER 1 – A BOOK ON . . . JURY NULLIFICATION?

THE LATIMER CASE:

Gary Bauslaugh, Robert *Latimer: A Story of Justice and Mercy* (Toronto: James Lorimer, 2010).

JULIAN HEICKLEN:

Julian Heicklen was arrested many times for openly smoking marijuana, as well as for distributing pamphlets on jury nullification. He has run (unsuccessfully) for political office as a member of the Libertarian Party. Apparently, in May 2012 he left the United States in disgust over repressive laws and moved to Israel (see www.examiner.com/article/rights-activist-julian-heicklen-flees-us-takes-refuge-israel).

SOME SOURCES FOR JURY NULLIFICATION:

Melanie Murchison's 2012 Master's thesis on "Jury Nullification in a Canadian Context" available online at: http://qub.academia.edu/MelanieMurchison

Clay S. Conrad, *Jury Nullification* (Durham, NC: Carolina Academic Press, 1998).

ON CONSCIENCE:

The source of altruism has long been a subject of speculation and controversy. Why should people help others when there is no tangible benefit in doing so? In Chapter 1 I argue that there is an innate human concern for others that we call conscience. It's not exactly a new idea. Adam Smith expressed a similar view over 350 years ago:

> *How selfish soever man may be supposed, there are evidently some principles in his nature, which interest him in the fortune of others, and render their happiness necessary to him, though he derives nothing from it, except the pleasure of seeing it* (Adam Smith, Part 1, Section 1, Chapter 1, *On the Propriety of Action* (1759)).

Where does this aspect of human nature come from? It must have some kind of survival value, and many have thought that feeling for others — empathy — helps build communities which, through cooperation and mutual caring, must have contributed much to the survival of early humans. But how exactly could such a quality have evolved?

Scientific answers to these questions are emerging in, for example, the work of Dutch scientist Frans de Waal who has produced strong evidence that a sense of empathy and fairness exists in primates other than humans (see www.ted.com/speakers/frans_de_waal.html).

See also research on a remarkable differentiated neuron called the mirror neuron, which acts as though actions being observed in others are actually happening in the observer (www.ted.com/talks/vs_ramachandran_the_neurons_that_shaped_civilization.html)

MARK TWAIN:

The comments by Mark Twain about Huck's moral dilemma are cited in *The Annotated Huckleberry Finn*, ed. Michael Patrick Hearn (New York: W. H. Norton, 2001), 154.

CHAPTER 2 — A MIXED HISTORY OF JURY NULLIFICATION
REFERENCES FOR THE ZENGER CASE:

An excellent and detailed discussion of the Zenger case can be found online as part of a series on "Famous American Trials" by Douglas Linder of the University of Missouri–Kansas City School of Law: http://law2.umkc.edu/faculty/projects/ftrials/zenger/zenger.html.

REFERENCES REGARDING FREDERICK JENKINS AND THE *FUGITIVE SLAVE ACT*:

Stanley W. Campbell, *The Slave Catchers* (Chapel Hill: University of North Carolina Press, 1970).

Mark David Ledbetter, *America's Forgotten History: Part 2 — Rupture* (Lulu Enterprises, 2008).

Charles Warren, *History of the Harvard Law School, Volume 1* (Clark, NJ: The Lawbook Exchange, 2008).

BOOKS CONSULTED ON THE DONNELLYS:

Donald L. Cosens, ed., *The Donnelly Tragedy 1880 – 1980*, Foreword by James Reaney (London, ON: Phelps, 1980).

Crichton, William; *The Donnelly Murders* (Markham, ON: PaperJacks, 1977).

Ray Fazakas, *The Donnelly Album: The Complete and Authentic Account Illustrated with Photographs of Canada's Famous Feuding Family* (Toronto: Macmillan, 1977).

Norman N. Feltes, *This Side of Heaven: Determining the Donnelly Murders, 1880* (Toronto: University of Toronto Press, 1999).

Thomas P. Kelley, *The Black Donnellys* (Willowdale, ON: Firefly Books, 1993). First published in 1954.

Orlo Miller, *The Donnellys Must Die* (Toronto: Macmillan, 1962). Revised in 2007.

James Noonan and James Reaney, *Sticks and Stones: The Donnellys, Part One*, Revised edition (Erin, ON: Press Porcepic, 1976).

James Reaney, *The Donnelly Documents: An Ontario Vendetta* (Toronto: The Champlain Society, 2004).

BOOKS CONSULTED ON TED AND ROSE BATES:

Pierre Berton, *The Great Depression: 1929-1939* (Toronto: Anchor, 1990).

Bill Waiser, *Who Killed Jackie Bates?* (Calgary: Fifth House Publishers, 2008).

REFERENCES FOR EMMETT TILL:

Again, as for the Zenger trial and all of the American trials referred to in Chapter 1, an excellent source is the work compiled by Douglas Linder: www.law2.umkc.edu/faculty/projects/ftrials/till/tillhome.html

There are many other sources available online, such as www.pbs.org/wgbh/amex/till/ and www.heroism.org/class/1950/heroes/till.htm.

REFERENCES FOR KAWAS NANAVATI:

Wikipedia article and attached references: "KM Nanavati v State of Maharashtra."

REFERENCES FOR GRANT KRIEGER:

The statements of Justice Chrumka are in the Supreme Court ruling *R. v. Krieger.*

(2006) S.C.C. 47 . The previous ruling by the Alberta Court of Appeals is (2005) ABCA 202.

Various accounts of the case can be found online.

FOR KRIEGER'S LATER LIFE:
www.cbc.ca/news/health/story/2009/03/31/cgy-krieger-marijuana-pot-quits.html

REFERENCES FOR PRITCHARD AND OLDITCH:
News articles found on LexisNexis Academic (key words: Pritchard, jury, Iraq):

Fifteen news articles: *The Guardian* (London) February 29, 2004; April 26, 2004; May 13, 2004; June 20, 2004; October 17, 2006; May 23, 2007; May 26, 2007; July 7, 2007; *Bristol Evening Post*, May 12, 2004; May 23, 2007; *The Times* (London) May 23, 2007; *The Western Daily Press* (UK) April 27, 2004; *The Mirror* (UK) April 26, 2004 (three articles).

COMMENTS ON THE O.J. SIMPSON TRIAL:
Despite the awful performance by the prosecutors, most of the millions of us who watched the verdict come down could not really believe Simpson would be found not guilty. I can't remember the verdict being pronounced, but I cannot forget Simpson mouthing the words "thank you, thank you" to the jury.

This trial was a shock to those who thought justice would prevail. Was this another case where jury nullification led to a bad verdict? It is difficult to know. The prosecution was so inept that it is possible that the jury was not convinced Simpson was guilty. The verdict then would not have been the result of nullification, which is when a jury knowingly releases a guilty defendant. They may simply have unknowingly done so.

On the other hand, there certainly were elements of nullification. For the mainly black jury, the sight of a black man being tried for murdering a white woman may well have conjured up images of lynching in the American South where black men (and sometimes young black boys) were killed for just looking at white women. The memory of these foul deeds and of many others perpetrated by whites on blacks and feelings about racist behaviour in the LA police force may well have created a circumstance where the jury saw an opportunity to balance things out a little.

There are interesting parallels between the trials of Till's murderers and the Simpson trial. The white jury in Mississippi refused to convict white murderers; the predominately black jury in downtown LA refused to convict a black murderer. This obvious problem of racism on juries will be discussed in detail in Chapter 8.

REFERENCE FOR O. J. SIMPSON:
Douglas Linder again gives a good account of the trial at
www.law2.umkc.edu/faculty/projects/ftrials/Simpson/simpson.htm.

CHAPTER 3 – HOW IT ALL BEGAN: JAILING JURORS
SOURCES FOR THE TRIAL OF WILLIAM PENN:
Borrowed from the Reading Room at the Penn Club, London, UK:
Samuel M. Janney, *The Life of William Penn* (Freeport, NY: Books for Libraries Press, 1970), originally published 1851.
www.shapirosher.com/pages/news/135/the-trial-of-william-penn.
www.1215.org/lawnotes/lawnotes/penntrial.htm.
Edited transcript of the trial: www.constitution.org/trials/penn/penn-mead.htm.
Original transcript: http://archive.org/details/trialwilliampen00meadgoog.

SOURCES FOR MAGNA CARTA AND KING JOHN:
Claire Breay, *Magna Carta, Manuscripts and Myths* (The British Library, 2010).
Full text of Magna Carta in English: www.constitution.org/eng/magnacar.htm.
www.fordham.edu/halsall/source/magnacarta.asp.
www.bbc.co.uk/history/british/middle_ages/magna_01.shtml.

CHAPTER 4 – MORGENTALER: NOT GUILTY
BOOKS CONSULTED ON THE MORGENTALER TRIALS:
F.L. Morton, *Morgentaler v Borowski: Abortion, the Charter, and the Courts* (Toronto: McClelland and Stewart, 1992).
Eleanor Wright Pelrine, *Morgentaler: The Doctor Who Couldn't Turn Away* (Winnipeg: Gage, 1975).

ONLINE SOURCES INCLUDE:

www.morgentaler25years.ca

http://en.wikipedia.org/wiki/R._v._Morgentaler

http://en.wikipedia.org/wiki/Henry_Morgentaler

www.law.ualberta.ca/centres/ccs/rulings/rvmorgentaler.php

www.thecanadianencyclopedia.com/articles/henry-morgentaler

Some details about Morgentaler's Ontario trial come from personal discussions with defence lawyer Morris Manning.

FINAL SCC RULING ON MORGENTALER:

R. v. Morgentaler (1988) 1 S.C.R. 30.

COMMENTS ON THE 1988 SCC RULING:

The 1988 Supreme Court ruling on abortion did not explicitly legalize abortion, but struck down Section 251 of the *Criminal Code*, the section that criminalized abortion.

Canada has never successfully passed another bill dealing with abortion, although in 1989 the newly elected Conservative Mulroney government passed a highly restrictive bill through the House of Commons, but after much controversy it failed (barely) to get by the Senate.

Since Section 251 was struck down we in Canada, unlike most other countries, have no abortion law whatsoever. There are about 100,000 abortions per year in Canada. Recent polls show that Canadians favour the right to have abortions by a margin of about two to one.

CHAPTER 5 – THE SUPREME COURT OF CANADA NULLIFIES NULLIFICATION

All information taken from *R. v. Morgentaler* (1988) 1 S.C.R. 30..

CHAPTER 6 – LATIMER: GUILTY

For more detailed story and full list of references see Gary Bauslaugh, *Robert Latimer, A Story of Justice and Mercy* (Toronto: James Lorimer, 2010).

Also see Kent Roach, "Crime and Punishment in the Latimer Case," *Saskatchewan Law Review*, 2001, Vol. 64.

ON MARK BRAYFORD'S COMMENTS:

Mark Brayford's words are from email exchanges I had with him in 2009. Brayford rightly felt highly constrained by the Supreme Court ruling. Was there anything else he could have done to make the jury more aware of its rights? In retrospect he perhaps could have alerted the jury to the mandatory minimum sentence, had he done so earlier in the proceedings. By the time the question regarding sentencing arose from the jury it was too late. By this time Justice Noble had ruled firmly, against the pleas of Brayford, that the jury would not be told about the ten-year minimum.

But there is a way this information could have been passed on to the jury. In the earlier part of the trial, in cross-examination of the police involved in the arrest, Brayford could have pressed them on what they said to Latimer, who had not taken them up on the offer to get a lawyer. Had they made the seriousness of the situation clear to him? It would have been a fully legitimate question, then, for Brayford to have asked the police officers this:

> *Did you tell him that this was a very serious offence and if convicted of murder he would be facing at least a mandatory ten years in prison?*

This question, ostensibly about whether or not the police had properly warned Latimer, would have alerted the jury to the all-important issue of mandatory minimum sentences. Was this knowledge actually crucial to the jury's decision? Brayford said:

> *Yes. I believe the jury was clearly contemplating a not guilty verdict because they suspected that Robert would receive an unduly harsh sentence if they did not get some meaningful say in what a fair sentence would be.*

That is why the jury asked about having a say in sentencing. Being told that they could, and being unaware of the mandatory minimum, they opted for a guilty verdict. And Latimer's ordeal became a lifelong nightmare.

It is easy in hindsight to say what Brayford should have done, had he perceived the need to do so early in the trial — that he should have resorted to the sort of verbal trickery mentioned above to alert the jury to this crucial bit of information. But should the fate of Latimer have been dependent upon such prescience? Should his future have been so severely affected by this omission? Or should it be easier to give such crucial information to juries?

CHAPTERS 7 AND 8
OTHER SECRETS:

The right of juries to be fully informed about relevant information in trials is blocked in several ways other than in regard to independence and nullification. Sometimes this seems justifiable, other times, not so.

As we saw in the Latimer case, crucial sentencing information can be withheld. The general justification for this is that the jury's designated role is limited to finding a verdict of guilty or not guilty. This normally should not depend on possible sentencing, which is the judge's responsibility within whatever legislated directives he or she is given. Normally, then, the sentence is not really of relevance to the jury. But there are situations where it is directly relevant, such as when a jury is contemplating nullification, as in the Latimer case. When nullification is in play, then the jury deliberation goes beyond mere determination of guilt; it goes to consideration of mitigating circumstances and the reasonableness of the law in the case at hand. In such a circumstance juries ought to be informed about all relevant information, including basic sentencing information.

The matter of giving out sentencing information is complicated by the fact that it is not always simple and may involve information that has been excluded from the jury, such as a record of previous convictions. It is not reasonable then for juries to be given a full disquisition on all of the possible sentencing considerations. But it is reasonable that they have straightforward legislated information, such as mandatory minimum sentences, information that will be known anyway by some juries, and not by others.

There are several other instances of information that might affect the verdict being withheld from the jury. Rape shield laws are an example where it has been reasonably determined that introducing previous history of a defendant can be unfair and abusive. In civil cases, information that a defendant has insurance to cover any liability has been deemed inadmissible, because such knowledge might cause a jury to feel cavalier about a settlement — that only the insurance company will have to pay, not the defendant.

Juries cannot be told about a previous hung jury in the case they are adjudicating. This results in inconsistent application of the law because some juries will know about the previous trial and the hung jury, and others will not.

Prior criminal records are usually admissible as evidence, although defence counsel can bring forward a "Corbett application" to exclude this information. This is allowable when the judge feels that the information would unduly prejudice the jury against the defendant.

ON THE MEANING OF "DEFENCE":

My use of "defence" here will be contested by some lawyers, because it is using the word in a slightly different sense than the way in which it is usually used in legal circles. In court, a defence is taken to be the strategy that is used to contest the charges against a defendant, either arguments directly challenging the validity of the prosecution's claims or the setting forth of completely different claims that conflict with those of the prosecution (affirmative defence). Appealing for nullification is not usually considered a defence because it is not challenging the facts presented by the prosecution.

However, it is a defence in a larger sense. The online Farlex legal dictionary defines a legal defence as:

> *The totality of facts, laws and contentions presented by the party against whom a civil action or criminal prosecution is instituted in order to defeat or diminish the plaintiff's cause of action or the prosecutor's case.*

Normally this entails the challenging of facts or presenting of alternative possibilities, as mentioned above. But the actual definition of defence does not exclude other possible reasons for defeating or diminishing the prosecutor's case. It refers to "the totality of facts, laws and contentions" used to defeat or diminish a prosecutors' case. A defence lawyer could defeat a charge with a contention similar to what Manning used for Morgentaler (see Chapters 4 and 5) — not that the charge against Morgentaler was wrong but that it would be unjust to convict him. Such a contention is indeed a defence — a reason to defeat the prosecutor's case.

Quote by David L Bazelon at the beginning of Chapter 8: from the Dougherty Appeal judgment (see below).

THE DOUGHERTY APPEAL CASE:

In his 1988 Morgentaler decision, Justice Dickson heavily relied upon the majority opinion in this American case, by judges Leventhal and Adams (written by Leventhal). Dickson claims that the idea of juries having no right to be told about their power to nullify is "stated clearly" in the Dougherty ruling. The ruling is apparently the basis for the current Canadian prohibition on informing juries about the possibility of nullification. Let us then have a critical look what is argued, about nullification, in *United States v. Dougherty*. 473 F.2d 1113 (D.C. Ct. App. 1972).:

> **The idea that juries can be informed about nullification is an "old rule" and a "singular relic."** Supposedly there was need for nullification when the country (the US) was young and still under the influence of Britain, but once it matured and developed confidence in its legal system and laws, nullification was no longer necessary. This argument simply misses the point of nullification. As argued in Chapter 7, it is a long-standing and honourable cornerstone of the jury system that has nothing directly to do with early US history.

> **Awarding acquittals "in the teeth of both law and facts" is "assumption of a power which they [juries] had no right to exercise."** This argues that juries have no business nullifying the law. But even most critics allow that it is their business if they wish it to be. And as argued in Chapters 7, 8, and 9, juries have no purpose if they lose right to nullify.

The "so-called right of jury nullification is put forward in the name of liberty and democracy," but in fact "risks anarchy." I deal with this chestnut of an argument in Chapter 8.

Advocates of jury nullification assume that it will not be used "significantly or obnoxiously," but how do they know this? Again, I deal with this at some length in Chapter 8.

Juries should arrive at the idea of nullification without knowing they can do so — only then will it be genuine. See this point discussed at length in Chapter 8.

Juries are aware, anyway, that their prerogatives extend beyond the instructions given to them in court; those formal instructions are added to by "informal communication from the total culture" which is adequate to inform them of jury independence. This odd point, contradicting the previous one, is not borne out by facts. No one on Latimer's jury appeared to know about nullification. Many people I have talked to about it, even well-educated people and some lawyers, know little or nothing about it.

The dangers of excess rigidity caused by juries not being informed of their prerogatives regarding nullification is less "than the danger of removing the boundaries of constraint" that would occur if they were informed. This unleashing-of-the-dogs concern is similar to the one about anarchy.

Allowing jurors to assume this greater role would threaten the courts with paralysis. But there is little evidence that nullification, if openly acknowledged, would be used in a profligate manner. See Chapter 8 for a specific and detailed analysis of this point.

Compelling jurors to "assume the burdens of mini-legislators or judges"

by circumventing the law puts an undue strain on jurors. The argument is that knowing about nullification means that jurors will realize that in finding a defendant guilty they really did not have to do so. It is easier on them, this argument goes, if they think they had no choice. The knowledge creates "an extreme burden for the juror's psyche." A juror is better off if he or she can just tell "friends and neighbours that he [or she] was merely following instructions of the court." Apparently this is more important than making an unjust conviction.

It is better for the "sound conduct of government" to have areas like this where "logic" does not prevail and exceptions to rules are not explicitly spelled out. I admit that I do not know what this odd statement means.

"What makes for health as an occasional medicine would be disastrous as a daily diet." In other words, juries should not be told they can nullify because then they would, disastrously, do it all the time. But, as pointed out in Chapter 8, this is not a reasonable concern.

There is no real case against nullification or informing juries in this ruling. It is astonishing that Dickson made his landmark decision by relying on this shabby analysis by judges Leventhal and Adams, especially since in the very same ruling the most senior judge, the distinguished Chief Judge David L. Bazelon, disagreed drastically with the views of his two more junior colleagues. Bazelon's comments are direct and refreshing, especially after wading through the obscure and at times foolish prose of the majority judgment. One wonders if Dickson even read Bazelon's dissent.

Bazelon writes that in suppressing information about nullification we are "scoffing at the rationale that underlies the right to jury trial in criminal cases, and belittling some of the most legendary episodes in our political and jurisprudential history."

Then, regarding barring a defence counsel from raising the issue of nullification in argument before the jury, he writes:

I see no justification for, and considerable harm in, this deliberate lack of candor . . . Nullification is not a "defense" recognized by law, but rather a mechanism that permits a jury, as community conscience, to disregard the strict requirements of law where it finds that those requirements cannot justly be applied in a particular case. Yet the impact of the judge's instruction, whatever his intention, was almost surely to discourage the jury from measuring the defendants' action against community concepts of blameworthiness.

Bazelon goes on to point out the absurdity of having a doctrine such as jury nullification that has a positive effect in seeking justice but:

. . . at the same time . . . must not only be concealed from the jury, but also effectively condemned in the jury's presence. Plainly, the justification for this sleight-of-hand lies in a fear that an occasionally noble doctrine will, if acknowledged, often be put to ignoble and abusive purposes — or, to borrow the Court's phrase, will "run the risk of anarchy.

But, Bazelon writes, he is "unable to see a connection."

Bazelon proceeds to trash the majority's position on nullification, in compelling and clear language; it is tempting to repeat it in full here. Bazelon's statement on nullification is the finest I have come across. The above excerpts, and those in Chapter 8, are enough to call into even more serious question the basis for Dickson's far-reaching and highly unfortunate Canadian ruling on jury nullification.

The full Dougherty Appeal judgment is on line at
http://constitution.org/usfc/fc/473/USvDougherty1972.html.

OTHER REFERENCES CONSULTED FOR CHAPTERS 7 AND 8:

James Ostrowski, "The Rise and Fall of Jury Nullification," *Journal of Libertarian Studies*, Volume 15, No. 2 (Spring 2001).

Christopher Nowlin, "The Real Benefit of Trial by Jury for an Accused Person in Canada," 53 *Crim. L. Q.* 290 (2007-2008).

The US Supreme Court statement on *habeas corpus* is at *Brown vs Allen, 344 U.S.*

443, 512, 1952, Justice Frankfurter.

Following an op-ed article in *The New York Times* about the arrest of Julian Heicklen (see Chapter 1), there were 135 letters posted online. These letters contained versions of most of the American arguments for and against nullification. The article and the letters can be found in the *New York Times Archive* for December 12, 2011.

LYSANDER SPOONER:

Lysander Spooner was a nineteenth-century American intellectual, abolitionist, and legal theorist. He wrote many works including the one referred to in Chapter 8, *An Essay on Trial by Jury*. It is online at www.lysanderspooner.org/node/35.

CHICAGO JURY PROJECT:

The Chicago Jury Project was an investigation of the role and functions of juries in the US legal system, conducted by the University of Chicago Law School in the 1950s and '60s. The information reported in Chapter 8 was found at www.lawlink. nsw.gov.au/lrc.nsf/pages/DP12CHP9.

CHAPTER 9 – WHAT CAN JURORS DO? WHAT CAN YOU DO?
JURIES AS CEREMONIAL ENTITIES:

For other commentators' comments on this matter see Justice Fish (page 55), Christopher Nowlin (page 140), and Justice Bazelon (page 202).

NULLIFICATION IN THE UNITED STATES:

Patrick Barone and Brittani N. Baldwin, "Independent Juries: Liberty's Last Defense," *The Champion*, December 2012.

NEW HAMPSHIRE DECISION:

policymic.com/articles/10603/jury-nullification-in-new-hampshire-becomes-reality

American court rulings regarding the crackdown on jurors in California: see Ostrowski above.

LAURA KRIHO:

As one other example of American courts cracking down on nullification, this is a story from Colorado. In 1996, Laura Kriho, a thirty-four-year-old research assistant at the University of Colorado, was prosecuted for failing to reveal during questioning of prospective jurors that she had been arrested thirteen years earlier for possession of a banned substance. Kriho correctly answered all twenty-five questions put to her in the screening process but was charged essentially because she did not answer a question she was not asked.

After being selected as a jury member, Kriho refused to convict a nineteen-year-old girl for possession of methamphetamine, which would have sent the teenager to a Colorado prison for several years. A fellow jury member reported her stand on nullifying the law to the judge, who declared a mistrial. Kriho herself was then tried and convicted of criminal contempt of court. See
www.apfn.org/thewinds/1998/09/jury_nullification.html.

OTHER SOURCES FOR ARGUMENTS IN CHAPTER 9:

Regina Schuller and Neil Vidmar, "The Canadian Criminal Jury," *Chicago-Kent Law Review*, Vol 86:2.
www.scholarship.law.duke.edu/cgi/viewcontent.cgi?article=3003&
context=faculty_scholarship&sei-redir=1&referer=http
Case where a judge's refusal to allow challenges in jury selection was overturned:
R. v. Williams (1998) 1 S.C.R. 1128

INFORMATION ON JURY SELECTION:

Criminal Code of Canada, Empanelling Jury, Sections 631 to 644.
www.cbc.ca/news/background/pickton/qa-juryduty.html.

JUSTICE DICKSON AND *OBITER DICTA*:

Some people I have talked to question how binding Dickson's ruling really is. What if a lawyer simply chose to defy it? Dickson's comments were not central to the Morgentaler ruling; such a legal aside is called "*obiter dictum*."

The extent to which *obiter dicta* from the Supreme Court are binding is in some dispute. The matter was seemingly resolved in a 1980 ruling, *R. v. Sellars* (1980) 1 S.C.R. 527 — a ruling initially written in French. A subsequent English translation included the phrase "this is the interpretation that must prevail," referring to the opinion that all *obiter dicta* from the Supreme Court are binding on all subsequent decisions by lower courts. Moreover, legal notes describing the Sellars ruling emphasized this apparent decision that *obiter dicta* from the Supreme Court would henceforth be binding.

However, a subsequent SCC ruling, *R. v. Henry,* (2005) SCC 76, disputes that interpretation. Moreover, Justice Douglas Lambert of the BC Court of Appeal, writing extra-judicially, claimed that the confusion in the Sellars ruling arose from a translation error, that "must prevail" actually should have read "should prevail." The difference is that in the former would make *obiter dicta* binding, while the latter would not. See Douglas Lambert, "Ratio Decidendi and Obiter Dicta" (1993), 52 *Advocate* (BC) 689.

The current situation is summed up in a Canadian legal manual, *The Essential GAAR Manual: Policies, Principles and Procedures*, 2006. On page 161 the manual states:

> *Although the issue is not settled, it appears that obiter dictum of the Supreme Court of Canada is at least highly persuasive on lower courts, if not binding . . .*

So it seems that a Supreme Court *obiter dictum*, though not to be lightly dismissed, is not necessarily binding. Where does this leave us with Justice Dickson? Clearly his nullification statement was *obiter dictum;* it was beside the point of the main ruling, and Dickson himself describes his jury nullification comments in a way that suggest they were, in fact, *obiter dictum:*

> *Although my disposition of the appeal makes it unnecessary, strictly speaking, to review Mr. Manning's argument before the jury, I find the argument so troubling that I feel compelled to comment.*

Dickson's comments by themselves might be considered non-binding, but the Supreme Court ruling on Latimer complicates the picture. The Court in Latimer's case wrote:

> *68 — The appellant's second argument is a broad one, that the accused person has some right to jury nullification. How could there be any such "right"? As a matter of logic and principle, the law cannot encourage jury nullification. When it occurs, it may be appropriate to acknowledge that occurrence. But, to echo the words of Morgentaler (1988), saying that jury nullification may occur is distant from deliberately allowing the defense to argue it before a jury or letting a judge raise the possibility of nullification in his or her instructions to the jury.*

Here we have a judgment directly related to the appeal that confirms Dickson's ruling and seemingly raises it from an *obiter dictum* to a precedent-setting ruling. It is not just an aside here, but central to the appeal.

Dickson's nullification statement, with its subsequent confirmation in the Latimer ruling, is certainly taken as binding by many commentators. Even before this confirmation in the Latimer proceedings, defence lawyer Mark Brayford felt he could say nothing about nullification to the jury (mentioned in my discussions with him). In Latimer's Supreme Court hearing, eminent defence lawyer Edward Greenspan allowed that, given Dickson's ruling, juries could not be told about the possibility of nullification. So the idea that nullification was to be kept secret was well entrenched by the time of Latimer's hearing.

In later writings, after Latimer, one finds common reference to the law now being clear on the issue. For example:

> *The law is clear that the defense cannot raise the issue before the jury. Morgentaler dealt with a section of the Criminal Code that restricts the availability of abortions. The defense advised jurors that, if they did not like the law, they need not enforce it. The court said that addressing the jury in this manner would disturb and undermine the jury system.*

(See www.treatingyourself.com/vbulletin/archive/index.php?t-24597.html.) And:

> . . . *our law strictly prohibits either the trial judge or the lawyers from telling jurors about the ultimate power that they always in fact possess to nullify a prosecution by simply returning a not guilty verdict.*

(See James Stribopoulos, "A Primer on Jury Nullification." Jan. 23, 2007. http://juror.ca/article_5.htm.)

Are we to take Dickson's nullification statement as having the force of a legal precedent, then? Probably. But given that his original words were *obiter dictum*, perhaps it is possible to argue in some way that they need not be binding. If so, there might be an opening for a brave lawyer to challenge Dickson by presenting a nullification defence and hoping that he or she can get far enough to bring a Constitutional challenge into play. That is where the case could have some traction (see Constitutional argument, Chapter 7).

The problems start with the fact that the judge can declare a mistrial if it is suspected that the defence lawyer's comments have prejudiced the jury, and given most judges' feelings about nullification it is quite likely that any direct reference to the possibility would cause many judges to call an immediate mistrial. It is also possible that the defence lawyer could be held in contempt of court for disrespecting the authority of the judge.

Maybe some clever lawyer will figure out a way through this legal maze and challenge Dickson's ruling.

BIBLIOGRAPHY

Abortion Rights Coalition of Canada. "The Morgentaler Decision: A 25th Anniversary Celebration." www.morgentaler25years.ca.

Alberta Law Foundation. "R. v. Morgentaler." http://www.law.ualberta.ca/centres/ccs/rulings/rvmorgentaler.php.

"American Judges Accused of Jury Tampering: Juries Nullified Over Jury Nullification." *APFN*, July 9, 1998. www.apfn.org/thewinds/1998/09/jury_nullification.html.

Barone, P. and B. N. Baldwin. "Independent Juries: Liberty's Last Defense." *The Champion* (December 2012).

Bauslaugh, G. *Robert Latimer: A Story of Justice and Mercy*. Toronto: James Lorimer & Company, 2010.

Berton, P. *The Great Depression: 1929-1939*. Toronto: Anchor, 1990.

Bingham, T. *The Rule of Law*. London: Allen Lane, 2010.

Bowman, John. "Q&A: Selecting a jury for the Pickton trial." *cbc.ca*, December 3, 2007. www.cbc.ca/news/background/pickton/qa-juryduty.html.

Breay, C. *Magna Carta, Manuscripts and Myths*. London: The British Library, 2010.

Bristol Evening Post, May 12, 2004; May 23, 2007.

Brown v. Allen, 344 (U.S. 1952).

Campbell, S. W. *The Slave Catchers*. Chapel Hill: University of North Carolina Press, 1970.

Canadian Press, The. "Activist for medical marijuana gives up crusade." *cbc.ca*, March 31, 2009. www.cbc.ca/news/health/story/2009/03/31/cgy-krieger-marijuana-pot-quits.html.

Conrad, C. S. *Jury Nullification*. Durham, North Carolina: Carolina Academic Press, 1998.

Cosens, D. L. (ed.) *The Donnelly Tragedy 1880 – 1980*. Foreword by James Reaney. London, ON: Phelps, 1980.

Crichton, W. *The Donnelly Murders*. Markham, ON: PaperJacks, 1977.

Criminal Code of Canada. Empanelling Jury, s. 631 to 644.

Devlin, P. *Trial by Jury*. London: Stevens and Sons, 1956.

Essential GAAR Manual: Policies, Principles and Procedures, The. 2006.

Fazakas, R. *The Donnelly Album: The Complete and Authentic Account Illustrated with Photographs of Canada's Famous Feuding Family*. Toronto: Macmillan, 1977.

Feltes, N. N. *This Side of Heaven: Determining the Donnelly Murders, 1880*. Toronto: University of Toronto Press, 1999.

Ibeji, Mike. "King John and the Magna Carta." Last modified February 17, 2011. www.bbc.co.uk/history/british/middle_ages/magna_01.shtml.

Janney, S. M. *The Life of William Penn*. Freeport, NY: Books for Libraries Press, 1970. Originally published 1851.

Justice Denied, Issue 32, Page 34 (Spring 2006).

Kelley, T. P. *The Black Donnellys*. Richmond Hill, ON: Firefly Books, 1993.

Lambert, D. "Ratio Decidendi and Obiter Dicta" (1993), 52 *Advocate* (BC) 689.

Law Times. "Canada: A Criminal Mind: Juries Can Nullify, Just Don't Tell Them." *TreatingYourself*, 2007. www.treatingyourself.com/vbulletin/archive/index.php?t-24597.html.

Ledbetter, M. D. *America's Forgotten History: Part 2 — Rupture*. Raleigh, NC: Lulu Enterprises, 2008.

Linder, Douglas. "The Zenger Trial: An Account." Last modified 2001. www.law.umkc.edu/faculty/projects/ftrials/zenger/zenger.html.

Miller, O. *The Donnellys Must Die*. Toronto: Macmillan, 1962. Revised in 2007.

Morton, F. L. *Morgentaler v Borowski: Abortion, the Charter, and the Courts*. Toronto: McClelland and Stewart, 1992.

Murphy, Gerald. "The Magna Carta (The Great Chater)." www.constitution.org/eng/magnacar.htm.

Mutchison, M. 2012 Master's thesis on "Jury Nullification in a Canadian Context." Available online at http://qub.academia.edu/MelanieMurchison.

New South Wales Government. "Chicago Jury Project." Last modified July 22, 2013. www.lawlink.nsw.gov.au/lrc.nsf/pages/DP12CHP9.

New York Times Archive for December 12, 2011.

Noonan, J. and J. Reaney. *Sticks and Stones: The Donnellys, Part One*. Revised edition. Erin, ON: Press Porcepic, 1976.

Nowlin, C. "The Real Benefit of Trial by Jury for an Accused Person in Canada," 53 *Crim. L. Q.* 290 (2007-2008).

Ostrowski, J. "The Rise and Fall of Jury Nullification," *Journal of Libertarian Studies*, Volume 15, No. 2 (Spring 2001).

Pelrine, E. W. *Morgentaler: The Doctor Who Couldn't Turn Away*. Winnipeg: Gage, 1975.

Penn, William and William Mead. *The Trial of William Penn and William Mead, at the Old Bailey, for a Tumultuous Assembly: 22 Charles II. A.D. 1670*. Headley Brothers, 1670.

R. v. Henry (2005) S.C.C. 76.

R. v. Krieger. (2006) S.C.C. 47 and (2005) ABCA 202.

R. v. Morgentaler (1988) 1 S.C.R. 30.

R. v. Sellars (1980) 1 S.C.R. 527.

R. v. Williams (1998) 1 S.C.R. 1128.

Ramachandran, V.S. "The Neurons that Shaped Civilization." www.ted.com/talks/vs_ramachandran_the_neurons_that_shaped_civilization.html.

Reaney, J. *The Donnelly Documents: An Ontario Vendetta*. Toronto: The Champlain Society, 2004.

Reiman, J. and P. Leighton. *The Rich Get Richer and the Poor Get Prison, 9th ed.* Boston: Pearson, 2004.

Rich, N. "The Nightmare of the West Memphis Three" *New York Review of Books* (April 4, 2013).

Roach, K. "Crime and Punishment in the Latimer Case" *Saskatchewan Law Review*, Vol. 64 (2001).

Sandler, Paul Mark. "The Trial of William Penn." *The Daily Record*, February 9, 2001. www.shapirosher.com/pages/news/135/the-trial-of-william-penn.

Scalia, A. Kansas v. Marsh, 126, S. Ct. 2516 (2006).

Schuller R. and N. Vidmar, "The Canadian Criminal Jury," *Chicago-Kent Law Review*, Vol 86:2 (2011).

Smith, A. Part 1, Section 1, Chapter 1, *On the Propriety of Action* (1759).

Spooner, L. "An Essay on Trial by Jury." www.lysanderspooner.org/node/35.

Stribopoulos, J. "A Primer on Jury Nullification." Jan. 23, 2007. http://juror.ca/article_5.htm.

Suede, Michael. "Jury Nullification In New Hampshire Becomes Reality." policymic, 2012. www. policymic.com/articles/10603/jury-nullification-in-new-hampshire-becomes-reality.

The Mirror. April 26, 2004.

"The Text of Magna Carta." www.fordham.edu/halsall/source/magnacarta.asp.

The Times . May 23, 2007.

The Western Daily Press. April 27, 2004.

"The Trial of William Penn (1670)." www.1215.org/lawnotes/lawnotes/ penntrial.htm.

Twain, M. *The Annotated Huckleberry Finn,* ed. Michael Patrick Hearn. New York: W. H. Norton, 2001.

United States v. Dougherty. 473 F.2d 1113 (D.C. Ct. App. 1972).

Waiser, B. *Who Killed Jackie Bates?* Calgary: Fifth House Publishers, 2008.

Warren, C. *History of the Harvard Law School, Volume 1.* Clark, NJ: The Lawbook Exchange, 2008.

INDEX